Promoting
Quality and Equality
in Schools:

Empowering Teachers through Change

David Fulton Publishers Ltd
2 Barbon Close, London WC1N 3JX

First published in Great Britain by
David Fulton Publishers 1994

Note: The right of Ruth Frith and Pat Mahony to be identified as the editors of this work has been asserted by them in accordance with the Copyright, Designs and Patents Act 1988.

Copyright © David Fulton Publishers Limited

British Library Cataloguing in Publication Data

A catalogue record for this book is available from the British Library

ISBN 1-85346-343-4 ✓

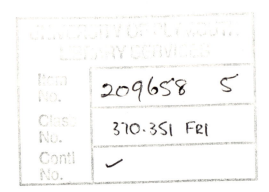
Typeset by Action Typesetting Limited, Gloucester
Printed in Great Britain by the Cromwell Press, Melksham

Contents

List of Contributors

Joanna Danischewsky has taught technology in inner city secondary schools for a number of years. She is, at present, pursuing her equal opportunities interests as a Head of Year in a boys' school with an all-male management team.

Ruth Frith has worked as a teacher and manager in both the secondary and further education sectors. She is currently Education Adviser for the London Borough of Waltham Forest with specific responsibility for Sex-Equality. Ruth also provides training and consultancy on a wide range of equality issues.

Rita Joseph has taught in the secondary sector in the field of Special Educational Needs. She is currently working with the Learning Support Team in the London Borough of Newham. In addition, she teaches with Elena Noel-Beswick at Dalston Children's Centre Saturday School.

Lindsey Lampard has taught for several years in the primary sector in inner city schools and has held the post of Early Years Co-ordinator. At present she is a successful class teacher in a primary school in East London.

Pat Mahony is Head of the Department of Educational Studies at Goldsmiths College. Included in her publications are *Schools For Boys, Learning Our Lines* (ed.) with Carol Jones and journal articles on equal opportunities and policy development in teacher education.

Elena Noel-Beswick has taught science and has been a Head of Year in secondary schools for a number of years. She has successfully undertaken many equal opportunities initiatives and at present holds a post as Student Support Co-ordinator.

Marjorie Smith is a Special Needs Co-ordinator in an East London primary school. She is also a researcher for an ESRC-funded project on Gender and Special Educational Needs at the Institute of Education in London.

Jennifer Walden has spent a number of years teaching in secondary education where she played a major part in equal opportunities work. She is, at present, a lecturer in Historical and Theoretical Studies of Media and Design at the University of Portsmouth.

Eve Wilson has taught English and drama in co-educational comprehensive schools since the early 1970s. She has always taken a keen interest in equal opportunities work and is currently applying this to her present post of Deputy Headteacher in a large comprehensive girls' school in the London Borough of Newham.

Elizabeth Young has taught technology in several secondary schools, mainly in inner city areas. Her present post is Head of the Technology Faculty in a school in Kent. In addition she is studying for a Master's Degree at the University of Greenwich.

Introduction

Ruth Frith and Pat Mahony

Over the last ten years the educational world has been completely reshaped. Those involved in it find themselves reeling under the pressure of having to manage a rapid rate of change dictated by a welter of new legislation introduced at breathtaking speed. At grass roots level, teachers are faced with a constant redirection of their everyday practice. Governors now find themselves as Boards of Directors, Headteachers as Business Unit Managers and Parents are the focus of marketing in their role as consumers. Teachers implement the business plan, Local Education Authority (LEA) officers and advisers are preparing to join other companies or await the bailiffs and each pupil carries a price on her/his head.

As well as the change in the relationships between those who manage education, the funding and management of schools has been altered, the content of the curriculum laid down by central government, modes of assessment radically changed and a moral panic about falling standards maintained at a time of increased levels of achievement.

It is little wonder that practitioners have found it difficult to develop and implement new initiatives in the area of Equality of Opportunity. For those who are positive about the development of Equality of Opportunity, it often seems like just one more agenda item on an already impossibly long list. For those who have always looked for reasons not to address the issues, there is now the perfect excuse − limited time and more important concerns such as creating a quality school. But, what many have failed to realise is that quality and equality are inextricably linked. How can we attempt to raise standards through the delivery of a new curriculum and with new modes of assessment, without using the knowledge we have gained about the differential effect of teaching style and grouping on pupil performance? How can we hope to improve our assessment techniques if we ignore what we have learnt about differences in motivation and performance between girls and boys? How can we hope to develop productive mechanisms for appraising teacher performance without acknowledging the different ways in which women and men develop their teaching styles? The enormous amount of research that was carried out in the 1980s is not an old fashioned irrelevance, it was and still is central to the task of improving the quality of education.

Any school therefore which is aiming to raise standards and is not looking at issues of equality is bound to fail and those schools which are seemingly addressing the issues and discover that standards are not rising, should look again. Similarly, a school where teachers are given no professional development in how to improve their practice will be a school where staff morale is low and it will not thrive.

In 1990 the Gender Action Project (GAP) was initiated as a means of addressing some of these issues. In our respective roles as a Local Education Authority Adviser and a Lecturer in Teacher Education we came together, as project managers, with three major concerns for development. First, we were concerned that as the connections were not being made between quality and equality, the commitment to improving the quality of education for girls was becoming a low priority amongst educators. Second, many of the teachers we worked with in schools felt exhausted and battered by the ever increasing demands made of them. Morale was low and teachers felt disempowered and deprofessionalised. We wanted to work with teachers in a way which ensured that they had control over their own professional development. Third, whilst recognising the valuable insights gained from a large volume of research on girls and boys in school, we felt we knew enough about what the problems were and that it was now time to move on and explore strategies for change.

In the Summer Term 1990 the London Borough of Waltham Forest (see Appendix A) had seconded a teacher, Jennifer Walden, 'to investigate gender issues in classrooms and offer strategies to alleviate gender inequalities in them.' Whilst the report emanating from her work identified teachers in the borough who were aware of the problems and who were committed to eradicating them, she found little evidence that any concerted attempt had been made to improve the conditions of learning so that interaction between girls and boys in the classroom was more equal. A major recommendation of the report was 'for teachers to become experimental action researchers in their classrooms and see what the outcomes are'. (Walden 1990).

Implicit in this recommendation is the recognition of the necessity of engaging teachers directly in the process of change. This, of course, was not new. In 1985 Andrew Cant wrote:

3

In reviewing the experience of developing an LEA policy on sexism, the genesis of that policy and strategies proposed to encourage its implementation, there are grounds to suggest a possible re-think with a view to shifting the impetus for change from the LEA to the schools themselves. With hindsight the environment for change, that is the context within which both teachers and schools were working, needed clarification. It might well have been more fruitful to work through schools (perhaps on a pilot basis initially) rather than have sexism seen as an issue imposed from outside by the LEA. The process of identifying sexism within one's own school and devising a school-based policy offers the prospect of a whole-school approach which sets out the implications of anti-sexist strategies for all staff and for the school as an institution. Developments in Manchester highlight the fact that a 'top-down' model of innovation and change is in itself insufficient. While it is crucial for those in the field to feel their efforts are supported and made legitimate by the LEA's statement of policy, the 'top-down' model needs to be complemented by 'bottom-up' developments at school level. (Cant 1985)

The importance of engaging the attention of teachers in Equal Opportunities work and the processes by which this might be done was recognised and developed by other LEA Inspectors. The work in Brent involving collaboration between the LEA and the schools was an important step forward both in principle and in practice of working *with* teachers rather than *on* them. As Hazel Taylor said:

It is quite clear that if all pupils are to benefit from the anti-sexist insights and practice of a few teachers, then ways have to be found of extending it to many more. Equally, it is clear that simply requiring teachers to change their approach, or requiring them to discuss important policy issues when they are unprepared, or expecting them somehow suddenly to know how to behave differently in the classroom when it has taken those involved in the work many years of discussion, self-examination and trial and error to develop new approaches, is foolish and unrealistic. It is more than that: it is fatal. For the best way of ensuring that anti-sexist initiatives fail is to foist them on teachers (and others involved in education) without preparation or time to reach an understanding of the issues, and then be helpless in the face of things going wrong. The responsibility of in-service training therefore is to provide teachers with sufficient understanding and knowledge to make professional sense of the demands for change being made on them, and sufficient support to enable them to step beyond understanding into action in their schools ... Part of the in-service (INSET), therefore, must be the provision of a continuing follow-up of programme, and one of the functions of the trainer must be to foster the growth of support networks so that much of the follow-up work is taken on by the course participants themselves. (Taylor 1985)

As a consequence of this:

> Teachers became their own researchers and carried out studies in their own schools which they hoped would illuminate their and their colleagues' understanding of the ways in which gender differentiation operates. The insights thus gained would lead to action where change was needed. Data was collected ... examined, shared with colleagues and reflected upon. It generated discussion, recognition, amazement – and action. (Millman 1987)

There is no doubt that the teacher as researcher had many advantages:

> An attractive feature of using teachers as researchers for educational decision and policy-making was that it offered considerable scope for professional development. In addition to providing teachers with a clearer understanding of gender issues, school-based research was directed towards developing a range of observational and appraisal techniques which were likely to sharpen teachers' reactions to and understanding of other areas of school life. Another advantage was that the research process itself was likely to heighten self-awareness and reflection not only for the teacher-researcher but for other teachers and colleagues working alongside. (ibid)

But there were also a number of limitations. First, those of us committed to this notion of the teacher as researcher on the grounds that it was a significant advance on top-down models of innovation, assumed wrongly that awareness or discovery of the issues really would of itself lead to change. But there is no necessary connection between knowing what is wrong and being able to put it right. Second, even where teachers had changed their practice, could we say that those changes brought any improvement in the quality of girls' educational experiences in every case? We are not suggesting that in general innovative anti-sexist work had made things worse, even though in one case there was some evidence that it had. For example, the following conversation took place in a science laboratory where a young student teacher was being supervised:

> Karen: 'Ere Miss are you a sexist?
> PM (playing for time): Em ... what do you mean?
> Karen's friend: No Karen you mean the other one, not sexist, feminist.
> PM: Yes.
> Karen: Well tell her Miss, she keeps saying we're sexist because we won't work with the boys.
> PM: Why won't you?
> Karen: They keep messing up the experiment and we can't get a turn on the microscope. They think they're the only ones that can do it. Will you tell her?' (Mahony 1989)

What was worrying about the subsequent conversation with the girls was their total opposition to 'sexism' ever having been put on the agenda in the mixed class. Their objections were twofold. First they were heartily sick of the way boys had appropriated the term 'sexist' and were using it at every available opportunity to get their own needs met. Second, they were angry at being constantly defined as 'the problem'. They felt criticised for being insufficiently assertive and for not being interested enough in technological subjects. No one 'had a go at the boys for being mouthy' and boys' attitudes to domestic subjects was clearly not an issue in the school. For these girls, 'equal opportunities' had made life more, not less, difficult, at least in the short term.

But, despite evidence that in some cases anti-sexist work had been counterproductive, the point being made is that in most cases it was not known what effects the work was having. Little evaluation of teachers' work was available so that a picture could be built about which strategies had worked and which had not. Furthermore, it is not even clear that a shared definition existed of what would count as success. What follows from this is that the model of teacher as researcher needed to move forward into an explicit model of teacher as researcher/innovator/ experimenter and evaluator. In other words for teachers to take as the problem not *how does my school treat girls and boys differently* but *I know that my school treats girls and boys differently, how can I prove it, what strategies can I try which will change things for the better and how can I know whether or not they have been successful?*

However logical or persuasive this account might appear, it was not from such an explicit starting point that the project began. As project managers of GAP we came to it not from an articulated position on the history or the analysis of policy and its relation to practice but from feelings of frustration. The LEA's report was a catalyst in helping to make explicit what we had felt as individuals working in different parts of the education system and our decision to forge a link between a local authority and an institution of higher education was born from a growing sense of impatience that for all our effort, little seemed to be changing in the classroom.

The many years of experience in teacher training which involved supporting student teachers undertaking small research projects, never seemed to get beyond generating more evidence about patterns of sexism in school which merely confirmed what had been known for ten years or more. This further evidence was valuable in the sense that students discovered and owned the problem but it was also wearying in its predictable repetitiveness.

Within the LEA context, the very nature of the work when reviewing schools and colleges, similarly demanded that evidence be collected, although it was often known in advance what that evidence was likely to be. Policies would be asked for and then sensitive questions about identifying good practice would follow. Committed teachers told of their hard work in developing policy over the years and how they were facing increased frustration at the lack of identifiable change at grass roots level. Day by day, classroom observation revealed findings similar to those which teachers had been reading about for many years. Consequently what was reported to them at the end of a visit was often not new to them. Appropriate strategies were proffered to change practice and then it was time to move on to the next institution. Not only was this practice disheartening and demotivating, it really did not move forward the theoretical grounding for managing change and progressing equality issues.

In short we (the project managers) were fed up with reinventing the wheel; the problem was that few of the strategies or 'solutions' being proposed to classroom teachers had ever been evaluated. There was simply not a culture in Britain as there is say, in Denmark, of teachers incorporating experimentation and evaluation as part of their professional identity. In fact, within the welter of imposed legislated change, teachers had been disempowered and assaulted as professionals.

And that is how we came to want to do something different; to work *with* teachers, to empower them, to help them establish research projects which not only identified a problem and proposed strategies for overcoming that problem but in addition, evaluated what was achieved and what was not achieved. Only later (see conclusion) did we come to understand that what we were beginning to develop was a model of curriculum change and professional development which could be initiated and managed at the level of the individual school. In the light of recent legislative changes in the role and power of Local Education Authorities, the delegation of budgets and the proliferation of schools funded directly by the government, the traditional ways of managing curriculum and professional development are unlikely to continue. Schools themselves will need to establish models of monitoring, changing and evaluating their own professional practice. Through GAP we discovered one such model which can be generalised to other areas of innovation. As we have already indicated, schools which fail to grasp the need to review, change and evaluate are unlikely to survive the 'market forces'.

In September 1990 The Gender Action Project was born from a gathering of teachers who attended a professional development session at the Teachers' Centre one evening after a busy day at school. From the very start, the interest, excitement and motivation of those teachers wanting to be involved was refreshing. Teachers wanted to know what to do and, if no one could tell them, they were keen to find out for themselves. Many attended other training and support sessions but this project was different in that there was no formal taught course.

Several small groups of teachers from four schools opted to be in the project and they began work on identifying what they wanted to change. It was interesting to note that we all thought we shared the same view of what the issues were. With hindsight, not only were we not in complete agreement about the issues, we were also certainly not coming from the same political and theoretical positions.

As managers of the project, we have had second thoughts about whether in retrospect we should have begun with a taught course. It was very difficult to weave in the necessary broader theoretical framework as issues arose. On the other hand, had we begun in a more formal way we could have been in danger of losing the energy and commitment of the teachers to start 'doing something'.

What we did share was an enthusiasm to move on. The group was keen to get started and we, the managers, produced the following action plan (see page 8).

As with any research project involving several people, all did not run smoothly. Headteachers came and went and teachers were promoted and left their schools. Despite all this, five projects from three schools involving nine teachers were undertaken.

Chapter One describes how a co-educational secondary school tried to heighten staff awareness to the extent that, and in ways which, would change children's behaviour.

The projects described in **Chapters Two** and **Three** concentrate on the theme of single-sex groupings for girls and boys in a co-educational secondary school. The aim of the first project was to support girls in becoming assertive in the classroom and to help them develop mutually supportive strategies for dealing with the behaviour of the boys. The second was to monitor the success of existing single-sex groups in order to find out whether single-sex grouping is a useful strategy for improving girls' access to the curriculum and achievement in non-traditional subjects.

Chapters Four to **Six** outline the ways in which one seemingly small project in a primary school can become a whole-school initiative and at

GENDER ACTION PROJECT

Aim

To identify issues of concern to teachers and explore strategies for improving practice, in relation to gender issues in classroom management and pupil achievement.

Stage 1   **Spring Term**

To research the nature and extent of the problems identified

a)   undertake observation
b)   refer to relevant literature
c)   make use of external support
d)   produce clear written statement of work so far.

Stage 2   **Spring Term**

To propose, plan and resource strategies for change (including statement of desired outcomes)

a)   set up planning meetings
b)   prepare resources
c)   make use of external support
d)   produce clear written statement of work so far.

Stage 3   **Summer Term**

To implement, monitor and evaluate strategies

a)   undertake group discussions
b)   undertake observations
c)   make use of external support
d)   produce clear written statement of work so far.

Stage 4   **Autumn Term**

To produce written report

a)   support colleagues in writing process
b)   make use of external support
c)   review by project managers.

Stage 5   **Spring Term**

a)   Share findings with wider audience

the same time show how a school can address issues of equality at a time of rapid change and in line with the requirements of the National Curriculum.

What all the projects show is that concern about equality of opportunity is alive and well, central to current concerns and initiatives, and manageable within the new context.

CHAPTER ONE

Change the Staff and see the Difference

Elena Noel-Beswick, Eve Wilson, Elizabeth Young

Introducing the School

Reed House School is situated in a north-east London suburb. Although it attracts students from the whole of the borough, its natural catchment area comprises owner-occupied 1930s housing and two large decaying council estates.

In 1985, the borough undertook a major reorganisation of its secondary schools and Reed House, which had previously been a junior high school catering for over five hundred eleven to fourteen year old pupils, was gradually to become an eleven to sixteen comprehensive school for six hundred students. In September 1990 the school finally had its first Year eleven (aged fifteen to sixteen) students and appointed its full complement of staff so that a third of the teaching staff were new to the school. The male Headteacher had retired the previous summer and during the autumn term the female deputy was acting Headteacher. A new female Headteacher was appointed in January 1991.

At this time the number of full time pupils attending the school was two hundred and eighty eight boys and two hundred and eighty three girls. The number of teaching staff was shown as twenty one women working full time and eight part time and sixteen men working full time.

Many of the staff who had been part of the developing school had an immense personal commitment to the promotion of equal opportunity, had done much work in their own classrooms and there was a general assumption of shared values. The school had a multicultural policy but no policy on any other equal opportunities issue and there had been no structured work on translating policy into practice.

This Chapter discusses work carried out on equal opportunities (gender) between Autumn 1990 and Spring 1992.

In the early autumn term of 1990 there began to be a growing feeling of unease among the teaching staff about many aspects of the work, behaviour and attitudes of Year ten and eleven students. Most seriously, some of the new (young) female members of staff complained of sexual harassment by male pupils. The senior management team of the school responded by setting up a staff meeting in which concerns could be expressed and from this an action group was born, which would look at gender issues in the school. Simultaneously, an individual member of staff produced a thought provoking and much discussed paper on sexism and sexual harassment at Reed House.

At the first meeting the Gender Action Group (GAG) shared anxieties and discovered that we all thought that staff (including ourselves) were not reacting consistently to what we perceived were the problems. We shared stories of things we had noticed happening which confirmed this. These included: a female member of staff telling a boy pupil: 'You're behaving like a silly girl'; a male member of staff in an anti-sexual harassment assembly openly challenging the woman teacher giving the assembly because he 'wanted to say what the boys were thinking'; a refusal by some departments to review blatantly sexist resources and an implicit assumption from some staff that problems encountered were those experienced by all new members of staff and were not specifically sexist in origin. We began to question whether the staff did in fact share the same values as we had previously assumed.

GAG felt that staff were at different starting points which had resulted in a failure to combat problems adequately and consistently throughout the school. Firstly, there were those who did not recognise sexism or denied its existence; secondly, there were those who knew something was wrong but not precisely what or how to deal with it; and, lastly, those who knew exactly what was wrong but had no strategies or confidence about how to deal with it. In other words, and perhaps in common with most schools, the problems had never been identified at a formal level before, and therefore had never been formally dealt with.

GAG decided that we needed to raise awareness of some of the issues which concerned us and we sought a forum in which to do this. We were allocated a one and a half hour staff meeting. We wanted both to inform colleagues and actively engage them in thinking about sexism in school generally. With enormous enthusiasm, the action group divided into smaller units and devised a large number of activities.

We began by asking teachers to look at how choice of language perpetuates sexist stereotypes and structures the way we see the world. Copies of the 'Genderwatch' (Myers 1987) material for monitoring resources were made available. It was also proposed that all teachers should pair themselves with a friend and carry out observations of each other's classroom practice to monitor gender bias (see Appendix B).

Finally, a group of staff assembled especially for the occasion and calling themselves the 'Reed House Players' performed three scenes which were based on real incidents which had occurred in school and which members of the action group had found difficult to deal with.

The first scene showed a teacher with her back to the class when a boy dropped a book in order to look up a girl's skirt. As the teacher turned round, she saw the girl hit the boy with a text book and punished her. In the second scene, a group of boys tried to involve a male teacher in discussing the relative attractiveness of girl students. The final scene showed an incident in a corridor where a small female teacher attempted to speak to a boy pupil which developed unexpectedly into a form of confrontation where he blatantly invaded the space in front of and above her.

Members of the audience were divided into groups and asked to discuss the nature of the problems identified and strategies for dealing with them. This activity was received very positively and encouraged lively debate with some useful strategies being suggested. It seemed to demonstrate why incidents which had been dismissed as trivial were offensive or threatening and, because in the last two scenes the sex of the teacher was especially important, it identified that there were issues of sexism to be addressed in the school.

As a result of this meeting, all staff agreed that sexist incidents should be treated seriously and initially a simple notice was put in the staffroom where incidents could be logged. A member of staff had been given a temporary enhancement for equal opportunities and she developed this form of monitoring into a sexist and racist incident book with clear guidelines for use and clear procedures for dealing with problems. This was successfully launched at the staff meeting a month later. Throughout the rest of this term, the use of the book and willingness to follow through problems suggested an increased understanding of what constituted a sexist incident. The evidence collected during this initiative demonstrated the extent of the problem and the fast follow-up response was important both in maintaining staff involvement and in highlighting the fact that senior management were taking the issues seriously.

Although the initial staff meeting was extremely useful, with hindsight we felt it was also somewhat over-ambitious. It covered a large number of areas and they were perhaps too diverse for all to be successfully assimilated. Although some staff did take on board the brief work on language, to our knowledge the 'Genderwatch' packs have rarely been used: perhaps because we relied on staff reading them in their own time rather than giving them direct support, or perhaps because there is a need to be aware of gender issues in order to be able to use them. At any rate we learned that it is not enough simply to circulate materials without support, even if staff are committed to action.

At the time, GAG was also disappointed that few staff completed their classroom observations, indeed few of the action group did so. In retrospect, we believe this was not a wise starting point; although the exercise was a valuable one the timing was wrong and we had not taken account of how threatening some staff would find this exercise nor of the considerable demands it would produce on time in a busy term.

Gender Action Project

In September 1990, members of GAG became involved in the Gender Action Project. In the spring term 1991, Pat came in to school to meet with a small number of the group to formulate the aim of the project. This was agreed to be to support and evaluate attempts to increase staff awareness and bring about change in pupil behaviour using a variety of strategies. It was extremely valuable to have an outsider look at the work we had already done and give it a tighter focus.

This coincided with the time when our new Headteacher took up her post and with the inevitable anxieties that staff feel at times of such change, action groups became less of a priority. Consequently the group did not meet again until April 1991, and when it did it was with a slightly changed membership. As a group, we recognised that gender was not separate from other equal opportunities issues and decided it was an appropriate time to formulate a policy on all aspects of equal opportunities. This was wholeheartedly supported by the new Headteacher. The group felt that the process of writing and approving the policy would be an important first step in raising staff awareness of issues, and consequently planned a broad consultation programme.

Before we started work on the policy however, we had to develop some method of evaluating its success in not only heightening staff awareness of the problem, but also of the extent to which practice was changed as a result. It was agreed that there would be two principle methods of evaluation. Firstly, members of the group would interview all staff to find out about their perceptions of their own classroom practice in terms of gender. Secondly, statistics were compiled from the school's annual profiles which show students' performance in cross-curricular skills (see Appendix C). We were particularly interested in the ways in which boys and girls were differently assessed in those areas which research (Mahony 1985) has identified as being significant by resulting in girls receiving an inferior education. In particular we wanted to see whether the boys in Reed House did dominate talk in classrooms and whether they found it difficult to work co-operatively. It was reasonable to assume that if this was so, then boys gained more teacher attention than girls. We therefore looked at the profile components 'contributing to and following discussion', 'listening to and following information' and 'working in a group', as shown in the table below. This process was to be repeated at the end of the year. We were interested in these particular three categories because we felt that they would show evidence, if any, of gender typical behaviour. For each of the categories we noted down every time a student was 'cause of concern' in more than two subject areas.

A table to show percentages of boys and girls 'causing concern in three areas of classroom behaviour'

1) CONTRIBUTING TO AND FOLLOWING DISCUSSION

	BOYS	GIRLS
1. Does not listen	40%	6%
2. Reluctant to participate	24%	18%
3. Responses indicate difficulty in following the main points of discussion	12%	6%

2) LISTENING TO AND FOLLOWING INFORMATION

1. Poor concentration, fidgets chats or daydreams	43%	9%
2. Needs individual help and frequent repetition in order to understand instructions and information given orally	19%	5%

3) WORKING IN A GROUP

1. Unwilling to negotiate, wants own way	18%	3%
2. Little contribution made	21%	7%
3. Behaviour undermines group	38%	6%

Although these results are by no means scientific and are interwoven with numerous variables and contexts, they present a very interesting snapshot of life inside the classrooms of Reed House, especially as very few staff had recognised this imbalance in student behaviour.

When we analyzed our results we found that there was a wide gulf between teachers' stated perceptions of what was happening in their classrooms and their assessment of student behaviour. When interviewed, many staff acknowledged that boys received more teacher attention than girls, but felt that the balance was about 60:40. A number of staff volunteered that they did not treat boys any differently from girls and felt as a result that there was not really a problem in their classroom. A few staff said they thought they gave girls more attention.

An unexpected positive outcome of this work was the reaction of staff when presented with the table of information at a staff meeting: at last there was concrete statistical evidence that there was a problem in the classrooms of Reed House which had previously been grossly underestimated and this ensured widespread commitment to our work in this area. At this meeting, the policy which had been agreed in draft by the action group was presented to the staff and revisions were invited. A copy of the draft was circulated to governors. Subsequently a number of suggestions were received including some thorough and positive ones from hitherto unexpected sources. A final version of the policy was adopted and included in literature to parents and to new members of staff, and in the prospectus.

Although there was general agreement with the aims of the policy among the staff, they were still far from being realised in practice, so this had to become our next focus. We decided to look at those aspects of classroom talk which had been proved by the profiles to be of concern. At a staff meeting in the summer term and again at the beginning of the new school year, members of our group suggested simple and clear strategies (based on the work of the National Oracy Project) for ensuring non-boy dominated talk in class discussion which all staff could use comfortably.

These were:

1. Instruct pupils to answer questions only when asked directly. During question/answer sessions pupils should put their hands up and wait. A pupil should not correct another pupil who is attempting to answer a question. Pupils should be made aware of these simple rules before a question/answer session or class discussions. You might consider making a poster which states those rules clearly.

2. Allow each pupil plenty of time to answer your question. If necessary, give pupils an opportunity to write down their thoughts and ideas before you ask them to respond.

3. Encourage pupils who answer incorrectly. Help them to reach the correct answer by repeating or rephrasing the question or breaking it down into sections that the pupil will find more manageable. In particular, do not ask a boy to answer a question immediately after a girl has answered it incorrectly. This should also apply if an introverted boy has attempted to answer.

During the course of the project we evaluated progress by recording evidence of change, even when that change seemed not directly related to the aspects being worked on, since we felt it was important to see if staff awareness generally was being heightened. Some of the things noted included:

- staff pointing out that our cross-curricular sheets contained the word 'mastered'.
- a much wider cross section of the staff feeling confident in identifying and discussing issues of sexism and asking for strategies for dealing with them, for example, 'What do you do when the girls persist in stereotyping themselves?'
- an acceptance that all women staff will use the title Ms.

Evaluation – January 1992

Staff Perceptions

It is worth noting that in an effort to avoid the rather time-consuming business of re-interviewing the whole staff, we issued a questionnaire. Only five replies were returned despite persistent chasing. However, when we returned to our original plan to interview staff, colleagues were extremely keen to talk and offered useful and perceptive comments. This suggested (unsurprisingly) that staff preferred to engage with people rather than forms.

Each member of our group interviewed five members of staff. They asked colleagues:

- Do you remember the strategies you were asked to try in terms of generating non-boy dominated talk? (Prompts may be given if necessary).
- Have you tried them? With what result?

- What are your perceptions of your own classroom practice now and of pupil behaviour in lessons?
- Have you noticed anything else, positive or negative, in terms of general staff and student perceptions of gender issues?

All members of staff were able to cite at least two of the strategies suggested. Most staff said that they had tried particularly hard to help girls to answer correctly and to remember to avoid going to a boy when a girl had failed to answer and that the act of doing this had made them much more conscious of the imbalance of attention which they gave to boys and girls. Whereas in the initial interviews staff said that they felt their time was divided about 60:40 in favour of the boys, many said they now felt an even greater proportion of their time was given to the boys, but they were conscious of it and were actively trying to change it. However, they felt that the strategies had helped in making sure there was a better balance of attention given to girls in teacher-led discussion: the attention boys gained was mainly negative behaviour modification.

In their interviews, most staff were keen to offer additional examples of developments they had noticed or worries and queries which they had. This in itself is evidence that staff awareness has been raised. Things noted included:

- the new school prospectus for which the Headteacher had selected photographs showing girls and boys in non-traditional roles.
- the department which had refused to review its materials when the project was initially set up, put in a bid for money to evaluate itself with reference to equal opportunities (gender).
- the equal opportunities group was asked to monitor the new curriculum offer, and the intention was clearly stated that this should become its role in future policy decisions.
- the whole staff agreed without demur to the rotation of meeting nights in the interests of part time staff, all of whom were women and were disadvantaged by fixed evening meetings.

Several staff said that the project had been effective in both raising staff awareness and changing some aspects of practice, but that student awareness lagged behind. 'Sexist incidents are not any fewer, but at least staff are noticing them more and attempting to deal with them.'

Evidence from Student Profiles

The cross-curricular sheets are used every year to profile student skills, so in January '92 we analysed the same year group in the same 3 categories to see if there had been a noticeable change in student behaviour especially with regard to the specific discussion strategies used by staff.

A table comparing Year 7 and 8 with Year 9 results

CONTRIBUTING TO AND FOLLOWING DISCUSSION

			BOYS	GIRLS
1)	Does not listen.	Yr 7 & 8	40%	6%
		Yr 9	37%	16%
2)	Reluctant to participate.	Yr 7 & 8	24%	18%
		Yr 9	29%	38%
3)	Responses indicate difficulty in following the main points of discussion.	Yr 7 & 8	12%	6%
		Yr 9	15%	6%

LISTENING TO AND FOLLOWING INFORMATION

1)	Poor concentration, fidgets, chats or daydreams.	Yr 7 & 8	43%	9%
		Yr 9	30%	6%
2)	Needs individual help and frequent repetition in order to understand instructions and information given orally.	Yr 7 & 8	19%	5%
		Yr 9	22%	3%

WORKING IN A GROUP

1)	Unwilling to negotiate, wants own way.	Yr 7 & 8	18%	3%
		Yr 9	15%	6%
2)	Little contribution made.	Yr 7 & 8	21%	7%
		Yr 9	22%	9%
3)	Behaviour undermines group.	Yr 7 & 8	38%	6%
		Yr 9	33%	6%

Again, taking all the variables into account we noticed several trends.

1. While the number of boys reluctant to participate in discussion had risen 5 per cent, the number of girls had more than doubled from 18 per cent to 38 per cent.

2. The number of girls 'not listening' in discussions had risen from 6 per cent to 16 per cent, while the boys figure had slightly dropped.

One conclusion might be that we had worked hard for a year with the result that life in the classroom for girls had got worse rather than better. However another interpretation could be that these trends were positive steps forward. Perhaps it meant that girls were being noticed. As the boys and girls had discussion 'rules' to obey and boys were no longer permitted to hold centre stage, so perhaps girls were now being encouraged to contribute equally and where they were reluctant to do so, teachers now perceived this as a problem.

3. The number of boys suffering from 'poor concentration, fidgeting or daydreaming' had fallen from 43% to 30%.

4. The number of boys whose behaviour undermined group work also fell from 38 per cent to 33 per cent.

We also noticed that there was evidence of an increased general awareness of equal opportunities issues and of an understanding of their inter-relatedness: in staff interviews at the end of the project staff were keen to discuss other developments in school such as bi-lingual signs and publications and to raise concerns about pupils' attitudes towards sexual orientation and lack of staff understanding of the relationship of social class to educational achievement.

One other development within the school in terms of equal opportunities is worth referring to in some detail. A Head of Year post which fell vacant had, at the time of the final evaluation of the project, just been filled by the school's first job share. Members of the group regarded this as a particularly significant act of faith on the part of the Headteacher, not least because on one day a week neither of the two women part time teachers would be in school and because the nature of this role in school would call for excellent communications between the sharers. This arrangement was referred to by many of the staff in their interviews. This in itself was important since it suggested that staff had recognised that job sharing was an equal opportunities issue. All the staff who mentioned it were supportive of the innovation, and were extremely complimentary about the strategies employed by both the postholders and the school in order to make the venture viable. One of the sharer's perceptions was that this support for her appointment was general. She felt that where staff had reservations, these had initially been about how the practical problems would be overcome and might as easily have been directed at her as a relatively new and unknown member of staff rather than as a job sharer. These fears seemed to have been allayed even within the first few weeks of the women being in post.

A summary of factors which helped the project

Commitment by Senior Management
Both acting and permanent Heads were personally committed to equal opportunities and at different times and for different reasons gave

impetus to this work. It was probably also significant that they were women succeeding a benevolently paternal male Headteacher, since this created a fresh climate in which gender issues could be explored.

Allocation of Time

The action group was given time set aside in the school's meeting schedule for its own meetings and to work on staff development. This also gave status to the work.

Making a Small Start

We were prepared to start without first gaining the commitment of the whole staff. Once a start had been made, it snowballed.

Using Existing Resources

There was already considerable 'grass roots' commitment and increasing expertise. We found that the informal networking which we were able to do had a profound influence on change.

Building on Good Relationships

We were a staff with a tradition of working together and respecting and supporting each other on other issues, but also a staff able to have constructive professional disagreements.

Being Flexible as the Project Progressed

We realised early enough to change tack, that talking to people was more effective than circulating documents and we were able to regard failures as positive learning experiences and change tactics as a result.

Support and Monitoring

The outside, objective input, regular monitoring and encouragement were really important. The deadlines imposed by being involved with the project spurred on the work even when other matters seemed more pressing.

Evaluation

The evaluation procedures built in to the project provided motivation: it was possible to see that change was being effected and even when individual changes were tiny, collectively they represented a considerable shift in awareness.

Evidence

It was important that we offered evidence to staff drawn directly from our own school such as the 'Reed House Players' scenes and the statistics from cross-curricular sheets.

Problems encountered

- The pace of change nationally, locally and within school which made it difficult, at times, to maintain impetus.

- Accepting that no one system works for all time — the sexist/racist incident book fulfilled an extremely important formative and unifying function, but is now hardly used.
- Finding time for the project was always difficult: even with the availability of payment for cover, supply staff were not always available or it was not convenient to abandon our own teaching groups.
- Expecting too much, too soon — the range of issues covered in the first staff meeting was too great to be completely assimilated. We needed to drip feed and leave adequate acceptance time. The proposed classroom observations were both threatening to individuals and too time-consuming and were, as a result, largely ignored.
- Expecting automatic appropriation and acceptance of findings from published research (Spender 1982, Stanworth 1987, Mahony 1989). More proof was needed that the problems existed in our own school.
- Expecting less committed colleagues to work on aspects of this by themselves, such as reading and using the 'Genderwatch' materials (Myers 1987) and filling in and returning the evaluation questionnaires. They needed more hand-holding and firm 'persuasion'.

Conclusion

If we were to identify the three most critical factors leading to success, these must be: having support from senior management which is needed both to give status to the work and practically to facilitate it; the presence of a committed group of other staff representing a range of roles, experience and subject areas so that they can support each other and network with staff who are not directly involved; having clear purposes and deadlines to keep up the impetus of the work even when other matters seem more pressing. While we hope we shall be able to continue to depend upon the first two of these in future work, the third is something we may need to construct for ourselves for example by committing ourselves to attend a governor's meeting or planning a public launch of some aspect of the policy.

These considerations are important for it is clear to us that only the official project has ended, not the need for work on the issues since we are able to identify many tasks which need to be pursued if we really are to translate our policy into practice, such as:

- Professional development for non-teaching staff: midday assistants, support staff, librarian etc;
- the development of individual departmental practice;
- work with students to produce their own version of the policy;
- research into the complicated relationships between gender issues and other areas of equal opportunities;
- the development of other mini-projects such as the one on talk, to influence classroom practice.

And above all:

- keeping gender issues on the agenda: re-visiting old ground in cunningly disguised new ways!

Introducing the school in which the projects described in Chapters Two and Three were undertaken.

The Grange Park School is in a densely populated working class area with a mix of early century terraced housing and 1960s-built monolithic high-rise estates. The school building mirrors this with its mix of Victorian and added on '60s plate-glass. Currently the ethnic mix of the school is 51 per cent White; 21 per cent Asian; 15 per cent African-Caribbean; 3 per cent African; 2 per cent Turkish and a smaller percentage of Greek and Chinese pupils. There are twice as many boys as girls in the school and in some classes the ratio is greater than this.

Some single-sex grouping occurs within the school. This was chiefly instigated for demographic reasons, as in one particular intake the proportion of boys was considerably higher, which would have caused some very unequal distribution in groupings for practical subjects. Hence Design, Science and Mathematics initiated some single-sex grouping two years ago. This was continued the following year, but has only continued in Design for the current year 7 intake.

The school has 31 male and 20 female staff. There is a male Head and two female deputies. There is an equal distribution of male and female teachers in pastoral management. There is one female Head of Faculty (Design), one female Head of Department (Science), a female Head of Art and females in charge of Drama and Business Studies. All other senior and middle management positions are occupied by males.

Despite some females being in significant leadership positions within the school, we would contend that the school's ethos is nevertheless masculine. Askew and Ross (1988) have described some characteristics of all-boys' schools and predominantly male school environments in terms of competitiveness, authoritarianism, a prevalent atmosphere of physical challenge and what we might term *power through exertion* rather than negotiation.

Although such characterisations could not be applied wholesale to our school, they can be identified as aspects of its ethos. The strategies adopted by the vast majority of girls to negotiate the terrain of perceived male dominance, bear this out. Girls, for the most part sit with and wish to work with other girls in classrooms and are far less willing to work with boys.

Girls create their own girls' spaces within the school at break and lunchtimes and interest in the Girls' Club, set up eighteen months ago is decidedly increasing.

CHAPTER TWO

A Lesson in Single-Sex Grouping

Jennifer Walden

The following describes a short-term project involving one class of pupils in a mixed secondary school. The impetus for the project was the general concern, felt by a few of us in the school, about the learning experience for girls in the mixed setting.

The inequalities in the learning experience of boys and girls in mixed schools has by now been well documented (Spender 1980, Mahony 1985). A range of issues which affect girls in classrooms has been identified: the different ways in which the boys and girls perceive learning and their own achievements as learners, how teachers interact with these differences in ways which give more attention and positive reinforcement to boys and in effect confirm male dominance of classrooms, to the all too frequent instances of sexist and sexually harassing behaviour which are not only *there* in classrooms, corridors and playgrounds, but actually stamp and shape the *culture* of mixed schooling, thereby having a determining effect upon learning experience, achievement and teaching of boys and girls.

In May 1990 I had produced a report in Waltham Forest on gender issues in classroom organisation and management which highlighted the difficulties involved for teachers in dealing with these issues. The brief of the report had been to identify and report on good gender equality practice in classrooms. What I found through observation and discussion with teachers was a high level of commitment towards such good practice from a proportion of teachers in schools, but an accompanying acknowledgement of the difficulties in sustaining this and of working against the grain of male dominance of classrooms. The report offered some sound classroom strategies but made no pretence towards a magic solution to the problems.

Hence, determined to address the problem (but also under no illusions), I and a colleague embarked upon some further classroom-based research in our own school.

Getting started

Before my colleague and I arrived at our idea for the project, we had to consider carefully and speculate upon this climate and terrain and recognise the difficulties in taking on issues. We were particularly sensitive to the problem identified in research (Askew and Ross 1985) of inevitably focusing on the boys when it came to gender inequality in classrooms and the extent to which the aim to change classrooms to make them better places for girls ends up with even more attention devoted to boys in efforts to change boys' behaviour.

Our determination not to focus on the boys presented us with great difficulties in formulating a viable project. In the beginning stages the five teachers from our school who were keen to work on the Gender Action Project hoped to organise a single project to which we would each contribute. In a first rush of enthusiasm we met three times in October 1990, including during the half-term break.

However, despite lengthy discussions we could not come up with a clear project brief. This was mainly because the boys kept re-emerging as the focus of our discussions. Time and again we returned to boys' lack of cooperativeness in classrooms and their characteristic behaviours of talking over and interrupting others, dominating the physical space of the classroom, taking equipment from girls and misusing equipment, being competitive and verbally and physically aggressive with each other and with girls and sexually harassing girls.

We found our perceptions, valid as they were, continually returned us to prioritising work with *boys* as a means of 'equalising' the learning environment for *girls*. We saw such a strategy as being fraught with contradictions and misleading messages to both the boys and the girls and as such we determined that it should be avoided. That we were nevertheless unable to avoid some contradictions and 'wrong messages' will emerge later, as I detail the methodology and outcomes of our particular project.

The rest of that first term yielded no further progress in making our decisions. As more and more commitments in relation to our subject teaching, pastoral responsibilities, whole school issues etc. piled upon us, it became increasingly difficult to find time to meet. Discussions took place in odd ten or fifteen minute spurts at breaks or lunchtimes. Plans to meet in non-contact time were often thwarted by having to substitute for absent colleagues. A great deal of energy was unproductively used up in trying to find evenings or weekends when we could all meet up. A number of us were already involved in extra responsibilities and all we seemed to be generating was stress.

Nevertheless by February 1991, having abandoned our ambitions for one whole project, we formalised two projects to take place within our school. My colleague and I began work on our project.

The project outline

We opted for work with a Year seven class (eleven to twelve year olds) to which I taught English and for which my colleagues provided in-class support for bilingual pupils for two out of the three lessons per week. We decided to teach this class in separate single-sex groups for all their English lessons for a period of one month.

Our aims were focused wholly upon the girls. We wished to support them in developing coherence and mutually supporting strategies as a group of girls; to develop their assertiveness within the classroom; to give them a respite from the disruptive behaviour of some of the boys in the class; to affect in the longer term the quality of the experience of those girls in the mixed setting. We would pursue these aims through a specific method and content which would concentrate on raising the girls' self-esteem and give them space to share and discuss matters relevant to their lives as a way of building solidarity.

Clearly, as our priority focus was the girls, we had a less developed aim and strategy for changing the boys' behaviour, as part of our intervention, so the last, longer-term aim would largely depend upon how the *girls* dealt with and came to perceive the learning environment and the boys within it. We saw any change in the boys' perceptions and behaviour, as a result of our intervention, as being a *possible* outcome, although we had little expectation of such a change in the boys in such a short period of time.

We considered the *content* we would provide for the boys' lessons and chose a theme which we hoped would raise some questions and issues for them about predominantly male behaviour. More will be said about this later. What I will say here is that the emphasis we placed on the girls' work rather than the boys' in our planning, led to some further problems, as will be subsequently explained.

The class

The class was made up, at the time of the project, of sixteen boys and eight girls. The ethnic mix was; boys: white UK, four; African-Caribbean, six; Asian, five; Greek, one; girls: white UK, six; Chinese, one; African-Caribbean, one.

At the risk of labelling pupils, it is important to present a picture of the class. This picture will help to avoid the 'en masse' labelling that has almost inevitably occurred with the class in question, as exhausted teachers enter the staff room talking about '7x again' or 'those 7x boys', or '7x is a very low ability class isn't it?'.

Amongst the girls there were two friends who always wished to sit and work together. They were of above average ability in English and always remained on task and worked hard. They were lively and articulate and very good at role play and drama, although they would not volunteer to read or present things to the class and would not answer questions in the public space of the whole class. By choice they sat in the front part of the classroom, to the teacher's right.

Two girls, Sonia and Lorna, who used to be part of a group of four friends, had split off from the others during the second part of their first term. By choice they sat either next to or very near a group of 'extrovert' boys, at least two of whom the girls would sometimes call their 'boyfriends'. They were part of a group of boys and girls across the year group who were involved in 'having fun' and 'messing about' together. This involved them in, among other things, quite an elaborate system of contriving to leave the room so that they could meet up with those from other classes whom they hoped had also left the room and in devising various methods of passing messages to each other. Sonia and Lorna were of above average ability, very articulate and at the time of the project totally *unmotivated* by work in lessons.

One major concern was the very deep contradiction Sonia and Lorna found themselves in. I had witnessed and intervened in the designated 'boyfriends' behaving quite brutally towards them, pulling their hair, literally tearing their coats from their backs, emptying the contents of their bags onto the classroom floor, deliberately breaking their belongings. The girls seemed to be in a quandary. They were very upset by such tormenting behaviour, welcomed my intervention to put a stop to it, but were equally mortified if I applied sanctions against these boys, as if they had got the boys into trouble. This linked uncomfortably with the classic syndrome in our society whereby women bear the responsibility and guilt for the wounds inflicted upon them by men.

Of the two girls who used to be their friends, one had started attending school very irregularly and, although the reasons which had precipitated the non-attendance were not clear, it would not be surprising if at least in part, it was connected with the dynamics of the class. This left the other girl out of that original group of four, in somewhat of a limbo, not wishing to be part of the boy/girl culture, but not firmly established in any other friendship group.

Then there were two girls who did not really relate to the other girls in the class and had an unstable relationship with each other. One of these had learning difficulties and was acutely aware of this. She had little confidence in her abilities, appearance or social skills. She was further undermined through surreptitious though persistent ridicule, predominantly from the boys and very occasionally from the girls.

The other girl was also quite isolated from the girls in the class. She sat on her own or near the quieter boys. She oscillated between 'maternal' and 'young child' strategies. The 'maternal' strategy had its own contradictions of sometimes admonishing others for inappropriate behaviour and at other times, nurturing the daring and 'challenging' behaviour in the boys. Her other strategy was to play childish games with the boys which involved scribbling on each other's books and attempting 'pen fights'. Again this had its contradiction in that when the teacher intervened or the games 'overpowered' her, she rapidly swung to her 'maternal', organising, admonishing role.

Amongst the boys there were two very quiet ones, who themselves suffered the noise and disruption from others. These boys tended to sit, by choice, near the teacher's desk.

Three boys were talkative but non-aggressive or assertive. One of these was quite able and well-motivated, another was able but less well-motivated, one had learning difficulties. There were two boys who were bilingual with a small degree of competence in English. One of these had been involved in confrontations with other boys and had on occasion harassed one girl in the class by making verbal and written comments about her.

One boy was what might be described as an outsider. He did not mix easily with others and often declared his wish to work on his own, to do work other than the topic set or not to work at all. He would seek to change his seat more than once in the course of any lesson to avoid others, although very occasionally he would work with the bilingual pupils. He too was the butt of the muttered 'jokes' and intimidation by some of the other boys.

The other boys in the class fell into three groupings, two fairly stable friendship groups with two other boys either electing to work with and be friends with each other or floating back and forth between the two friendship groups from lesson to lesson. The two groups, by choice, 'took up their positions' opposite each other in the two back corners of the room.

There had been considerable and aggressive rivalry and competition between the two groups, usually instigated by individuals from each of the groups insulting each other and indulging in 'wind ups'. The sexism and indeed sexual harassment accompanying these insults was explicit. Apart from the plethora of 'your Mum . . .' insults, which, in spite of the vigorous defence they incite in the boys, only gave further licence to the idea of insulting women, the boys would frequently use the girls in the class as a means of getting at each other, implying liaisons and sexual attractions between particular boys and girls and otherwise setting the girls up in disparaging ways in order to insult another boy.

Both these groups of boys were very demanding of teachers' time, whether through continually talking to each other within the group or generally 'messing around' and making other types of noise or instigating 'wind ups' between the groups which would often flare up into confrontation, or disparaging the girls by talking over or interrupting their contributions, directly or indirectly insulting them or taking their belongings or sometimes their work.

There was a degree of difference between the two groups of boys which was to do with implicit and explicit behaviours. One group was more subtle in its behaviours and was more likely to *appear* to be staying just this side of the classroom rules. The other group was generally more physical and extrovert, constantly attempting to be out of seat or falling off seats, trying out the latest wrestling holds or karate kicks, invading the girls' desks for pens, rulers and other equipment and in particular instances, aggressively interfering with the girls.

They demanded and required more teacher time, and their classroom interactions were clearly *more* overtly disturbing to the girls. Whilst this group *evidently* dominated and invaded the girls' physical/geographical space, to distressing levels, the other group just as persistently invaded the girls' psychological space, through either disparaging the girls directly or using the girls' presence to disparage each other. This behaviour should not be discounted because it is perhaps potentially even more damaging to the girls in the long run and in being more subtly carried out was more difficult for teachers to control.

It also has to be said that while these two boys' groups had their differences with each other which could at times develop into intense confrontations, there was an implicit camaraderie of maleness existing between them. This meshed in with the apparently contradictory stance of intense competition with each other. There was frequent insistence that 'it wasn't me, it was him', 'Why are you picking on me, you don't say anything to him, do you?', but there were also times when confrontations occurred when all the boys involved would define my intervention as an intrusion on their male territory and patronisingly (sic) assure me that 'We'll sort it out, Miss, don't get in such a flap about it'. I also did not experience any of the boys, even those who demonstrated some involvement with two of the girls, 'crossing the line' and defending the girls against abuse and ridicule from other boys.

The project organisation

It was in this context that we wanted to focus our energies on helping the girls develop strategies which would empower them in the classroom and which they could also take into the corridors and playground. I prepared a scheme of work which was open to negotiation, but which would provide a framework for *sharing* ideas and experiences to develop cohesion as a group of girls; for feeling *positive* about themselves; for exploring some of the *contradictions* in their lives in ways which did not undermine their view of themselves.

Sessions planned in this scheme were: group games on saying things positive about themselves and each other; sharing talk and stories around favourite memories, objects, people, including bringing photos and objects to the lesson; a photo session, having fun taking photos of each other and constructing images; a walk round the neighbourhood talking about where they go, what they do, safety issues for girls and women, followed by making plans of their 'ideal environment'; constructing family trees and through this talking about family life; looking at expectations and charting 'cradle to grave' expectations of them as girls and women; looking at romance through pop songs, magazines, soap operas and literature; collecting songs, rhymes, sayings, poems about girls, including whole group dramatisations of poems and their own writing. Through this work it was our intention to create a context in which solidarity could begin to develop within the group of girls. It is my view that they could not have embarked upon such work in the presence of boys; the pressure of exposure to ridicule would be too great and I would not have contemplated such work in a mixed setting.

We spent less time planning work for the boys, for the reasons stated earlier. We took existing material developed in the Inner London Education Authority for anti-sexist work with boys (Askew and Ross, undated). We had contemplated using material which focused on early childhood and which brought in issues on how we are gendered into different roles, responsibilities, attitudes and ways of dealing with emotions, but we rejected this as we felt it called for too much abstraction and reflection and perhaps too blatantly required the boys to question their own self concepts. We also made an assessment, based upon previous experience of work with boys, that they would reject this material out of resistance and/or boredom.

We were also looking for a quick way to undertake the planning for the boys, as we were organising this whole project under a great deal of pressure, hence the reliance on pre-existing material. We eventually decided upon neatly packaged and highly structured material dealing with 'Heroes' and 'Violence on TV' (Askew and Ross). The contradictions between what we believed in and stated as our intention and what we did under pressure, will not be lost. We did, to an extent, foresee the problems inherent in such subject matter, although we did not resolve how we would strategically deal with it. How do you *question* stereotypes of the macho hero and the pervasiveness of violent images in TV and 'electronic culture' whilst at the same time filling the classroom with their favourite examples and thereby *legitimating* their standing in the boys' 'culture'?

Since we had so little time for strategic planning to deal with this problem, we had to rely too much on the strength of our own powers as teachers to raise questions, and our abilities to present a 'reality' which inserted contradictions and alternative desires and emotions into the seamless, wall-to-wall constructions of male identity through images of physical strength and aggression. This lack of suitable materials would have repercussions later. We recognised that had we had more time, it would have been preferable to prepare suitable materials ourselves. As we have shown, albeit briefly, there is a considerable need for good materials in this area. We also did not adequately discuss a *methodology* for teaching the boys and the extent to which we would also use the opportunity of the single-sex setting to tackle the seemingly intractable problem of developing cooperation between the boys. In planning the girls' work, method and content had been self-evidently inseparable, but the boys' work did demand a much more precise and self-conscious attention to method in our planning for which we simply did not have time. The combination of lack of time and the decisions we had made about resisting *extra* investments of time in the boys' work meant it was impossible to address these issues as part of this project.

Our work was to be further complicated by the difficulties we had in organising and being able to maintain the logistics of splitting the group, requiring as it did, two teachers and two rooms for three lessons per week for one month. The first major problem was that my colleague did not work on the school site on Friday afternoons when the class had English. This meant recruiting another teacher into the project. We found it difficult to make time to liaise and the chopping and changing between teachers led to a host of problems. We had not found enough time for all three of us to sit down and discuss methods and materials for the duration of the project. We had still really only discussed the overall scheme of work and this proved insufficient and problematic, given that we were changing over roles in the course of the week and had brought a third person in at a much later stage in our planning.

There were problems in finding suitable accommodation and as it was the boys' group who were the recipients of the change of room for the project, the double-bookings which occurred with monotonous regularity created a highly inflated sense of their 'territorial rights' and importance, as they sought to eject the other class from *their* room. We made a decision to put the boys in the different room. My normal teaching room was the 'gold-fish bowl' of the school building. Its wall of plate-glass window, like the viewing lounge at Heathrow airport, directly faced the main entrance to the school. The room was separate from the main building, annexed to the gym and sharing a foyer with the gym entrance. It was a highly favoured room with the boys in the school because of its private foyer, which provided a ready-made wrestling ring whilst lining up for entry into the teaching room, its easy access to the gym, if, by chance the gym door was unlocked, its tiny vestibule housing the doors to two adjacent classrooms, into which two classes of pupils would attempt to pour at the same time, providing wonderful opportunities for pinning each other up against the wall, and of course the constant diversions occurring outside the classroom window as visitors, deliveries, teachers, caretakers, pupils passed by. Hence, we were aware that, keeping this room for the boys' work had too many disqualifying factors. However, as previously suggested, changing rooms gave them the satisfaction of 'special treatment'.

We faced many problems of last minute changes to the timetable within a very busy examination period and within the period of the project, we suffered a staffing or room problem each week. There is much to be learned from this experience which could of course be seen as just a tiresome set of coincidences. However, such organisational 'slip-ups' can be extremely enervating to already overstretched teachers and can considerably thwart any successful outcome for gender equality projects. I shall return to some of these points in my conclusions.

Teaching and learning

We thought a great deal about how to introduce the project to the class and rejected many of our ideas when we realised their potential for reinforcing sex stereotyped attitudes. In the end we told the whole class that we were involved in a project that was looking at how boys and girls work and learn and what differences occur between their being taught separately or together. We did make it sound more attractive by suggesting the topics would be of particular interest to them, but did not go into this in detail, prior to the separation. We gave them details of the room change, but did not commit ourselves as to who would take which group. All the boys accepted the idea, given, I think, at this point, the fact of changing room. Although they liked the present room for all the attractions suggested previously, there was some element of special treatment in being given the different classroom, which boosted their sense of importance over the girls.

The two girls who were very involved with two of the boys and had, in a sense, disassociated themselves from the other girls in the class did not like the idea very much. They wanted to know more about our motives (perhaps wondering if it had something to do with their recent lack of work) and predicted that it would be boring with only the girls. When we spoke to them on their own we stressed opportunities it would give them to work on things that they were interested in and that they could complete without interruption. We did not focus on their personal involvements and the particular harassment they received, nor did we put things in such a way that might suggest they had a problem 'coping' with the boys, as we judged this would have undermined them further and strengthened their resistance to the idea. They listened to us, but we knew that they were not entirely convinced. The other girls appeared positively relieved at the prospect of being without the boys for their English lessons.

How the lessons went with the girls

The atmosphere in the room was immediately markedly different with the girls' group. They were comparatively few in number. It was easy to all sit round one large table, or form a circle of chairs. They were much more able to listen to each other and sustain talk through responding to each other's contributions. Nearly all the girls enjoyed the photo sessions, bringing in things from home and the family tree which provided the framework for a lot of discussion about families and their family lives. This revealed a great deal about the reality of their lives; the presence of male violence within the family, considerable difficulties in having to adjust to step-fathers, the everyday experience of their mothers and the complex reactions of the girls towards this which was a mixture of respect and blame! One girl was able to talk about her mother's death, which she had never done in school before. The two girls who were resistant to the project got involved in the family discussions and requested more time on this.

The two highly motivated, able girls talked voluntarily and at much greater length than they felt able to do amongst the boys. They were also great listeners and encouragers of the three other girls who had less confidence in their abilities or social skills. The girl who had been left in limbo when splitting from the 'boyfriend' pair became friends with the two bright girls. There were very marked changes in the two more isolated girls. The 'maternal/child' girl was able to drop these roles, although she became significantly more dependent on my approval, rather than the approval and positive reinforcement available to her from the other girls. The girl who seemed most lacking in confidence about herself became much more relaxed and happy and there was the beginnings of something like empathy and shared understanding apparent between her and the others, although again, there was a high level of dependence upon my approval.

The resistant girls still remained, to a degree, resistant, although one more than the other. The more resistant girl was absent for some of the sessions during the month of the project. The effect of this was to draw the other girl a little more into the group on those days when her friend was missing. She would then listen and be appreciative of others, did offer some contribution herself and did all the tasks set. She was frequently late for the lesson and wanted to sit on the edge of the group, as if she did not really feel at ease in the situation. When her friend was in school they would be even later for the lesson, would make frequent requests to leave the room, continually wishing to sit away from the others and when I urged them to remain with the group they demonstrated their continued disassociation through their body language.

The more resistant girl was also locked into some tension with the 'mother/child' girl, whom she did not like and whose comments she tended to disparage. She did really positively join in with the work on families. It was interesting that she made reference to the violence in her family life, with her mother and herself being on the receiving end of it. There was a marked change in her response in the last two sessions of the project, when she demonstrated a much more positive attitude towards being with the girls. I found out in the course of these last sessions that she had had a serious disagreement with one of the boys. I would suggest that this girl's position was even more deeply contradictory. It appeared that she had learned that behaving in certain ways afforded her some attention and appreciation from boys and men and she was dependent on this. And yet she was also aware of and lived, as a fact of life, with male violence.

How it went with the boys

In the absence of adequate time to resolve the many issues concerning the appropriate methodology for teaching the boys, my colleague organised a tight regime for them. They each had their own work-book with the twelve lessons consecutively marked out. They each had their own report-sheet to be signed by the teacher at the end of each session and counter-signed by the Head of Year at the end of each week. They were assigned a table each in the room, to be their work-place for the duration. (A table each would not be possible in normal full-class circumstances).

The boys were thus launched upon an individualised programme with external rewards, a strict, non-negotiable regime, designed for the purposes of *control*. Only once in the programme were they required to work non-individually, when the work involved interviewing a partner.

We had concerns about this individualised, control-led method because of its reinforcement of individualism, competition and working for extrinsic, rather than intrinsic, rewards, characteristics of learned male behaviour which facilitate and support male dominance. On the other hand it was difficult to see how we could teach them anything until their behaviour improved. The work on Heroes and TV violence had an immediate appeal to the boys, although not all of them sustained consistent interest. They did, to some extent, question the stereotyping involved in such images of masculinity, especially the more thoughtful, reflective boys, but it was a very fine line between this questioning and the opportunities the topic gave for celebrating such images. The report sheet system provided them with an immediate individual reward at the end of each lesson, geared as it was towards noting 'good behaviour'. This could have been developed as a means of helping the boys to reflect upon their learning behaviours. They also felt very satisfied as they produced pieces of writing in their work books, associating as they did *work* with *writing* and *drawing*, rather than speaking and listening.

During the weeks of the project I was aware from comments from the boys and the girls that the majority of the boys had assumed they were doing better and more important work than the girls and some of them were clearly still being as negative about the girls' work outside of the lessons, as they would have been inside the mixed classroom.

And yet, looked at in another way, it worked for both groups. Both groups, in general, gained and felt some sense of satisfaction and reward from the lessons. Both groups achieved, though they achieved differently. The boys' concentration improved, they paid closer attention to the presentation of their written work and they sustained tasks more successfully. The girls reached a level of articulacy in discussion and writing that they were not able to achieve in the mixed setting. Members of both groups (the 'quieter' ones in each case) felt relieved by the separation.

The evidence is inconclusive but, contrary to other research findings (Kruse 1992), the boys in some ways preferred the single-sex setting. However, we have to take into account their assumption of 'special treatment' and importance, the reward system and the short duration of the project. It also has to be said that in both groups there were individual reservations such as we have come to expect (Mahony 1989) about whether it was 'normal' to be taught in single-sex groups.

The aftermath

The pupils were aware that something different was going on in the different groups; questions about sex-role stereotyping had been raised; the boys had, in effect, been rewarded for writing about macho things and violence; I had spent more time with the girls; the boys had been under a regime, certain features of which were only practically possible in a smaller group. So, I was not at all surprised that in the immediate aftermath, when we returned to the mixed setting, the behaviour of the boys was worse. They had learnt about power and felt powerful and rewarded when learning about it. This seemed to increase the boys' interest in using their power against the girls.

The girls' solidarity *apparently* dissipated under this onslaught, but in spite of this certain features of what the girls had established remained. The girl who had been left on her own when the other two split, remained firm friends with the two very able girls. The other two girls, although not necessarily closer to each other, were individually more resilient to the boys, and the girl who occasionally depended on the boys, no longer seemed to require this. The two girls who were 'into the boys', remained so, but this was less predictable. Their defence of the boys was less automatic. At times they told them that they did not like their behaviour, although they felt powerless to stop it.

Longer term, things have more evidently changed. There are a number of factors in this. The teaching room changed to a room in the main building which has no distractions from outside. This robbed the boys of a further audience for their inappropriate behaviour. The more resistant girl moved classes, as too did one of the more extrovert boys. There were some subtle, but significant changes in the girls. They became more explicit in their rejection and disdain of the boys' behaviour and created a pocket of air-space for themselves within the group. The more resistant girl who remained in the class began to make strategic choices. In terms of doing her work, she sat with the other girls. She knew that was where she could get her work done. When she felt less inclined to work, or got bored she made surreptitious efforts to move over to talk to the boys.

What we learned

1. A Learning Experience for Staff

Overall, we learned that it is possible to design and carry out a project despite overwork, understaffing and administrative errors. The severe constraints on the time of the members of the GAP group and the lack of facilities in school to accommodate our needs were overcome in a variety of ways, some of which shaped the project itself and certainly the outcomes. The whole project was a learning experience for the teachers directly involved and for other staff open to learning from it.

2. Outcomes for Pupils

For the pupils the outcomes were positive on the whole. When I asked the girls recently for their thoughts on the project now that some months had elapsed, they all said they had liked it and would like to do it again. Despite our reservations about the way in which the project was carried out in respect of the boys, in fact, in the long term their behaviour improved and they achieved more. This actually supports an argument for single-sex grouping as being beneficial for girls *and* boys in the context of specific teaching strategies.

3. Preparation

The problems we encountered regarding the logistics of running the project, planning time, staffing, rooming problems etc. demonstrate the importance of getting all this sorted *early on*. It is vital that *all* who *need* to know about what you are doing know about it.

4. Support from Senior Management

It is important to try to win, and ensure that you have *support*, for what you are doing from senior management and especially that this support is not only in *principle*, but is *practical*. We would have found it much more helpful if we had successfully communicated with the Head and deputies *in the course of our planning* and had not just gained their assent in principle at the start of our deliberations. In this way, we might have been able to increase the value placed on the project and we might not have experienced such difficulties with the logistics of finding new rooms.

5. Involving Staff

We could have produced a bulletin about the project for all the staff. This might have won us a larger base of support. Undoubtedly, we would have had the cynical, critical and oppositional response, but there would have been supporters as well. It would also have publicly demonstrated our commitment to it and that matters in schools, whether everyone agrees with you or not.

6. Timing

With hindsight, it now appears that we might also have anticipated problems with timing. Was the beginning of external exams a good time or a bad one? It tends to be thought of as a better time to do innovatory work, but we have found that complications can ensue at that time of the year in schools, especially around those things of crucial importance to us, time-tabling and rooms.

7. Teaching Methods

We thought through some of the methodological issues at all stages of the project and attempted to anticipate the difficulties we might encounter, both for ourselves in adopting particular methods and with other staff and pupils in how these methods would be received. Our theoretical framework was based on what we knew about inequalities in mixed schools between girls and boys from current research in the field, together with our own perceptions. However we did not resolve to our own satisfaction a methodology which both controlled the boys' behaviour and challenged their individualistic competitiveness. Overall our approach was successful for the girls.

8. Success

Finally, whilst we cannot assume *all* girls or *all* boys will respond in the same ways and while not underestimating the complex ramifications of institutionalised sexism and how these are manifested and reinforced in boys and girls, nevertheless it is possible to organise and carry through strategic interventions which can have a significantly positive effect upon the learning experience of a group of boys and a group of girls.

CHAPTER THREE

There's More to Single-Sex Grouping than Girls and Boys

Joanna Danischewsky and Rita Joseph

History of the single-sex groupings

In the lower school, pupils attend lessons in their six form groups. The exception to this is Maths, Science and Design, which includes Home Economics, Craft Design Technology (C.D.T.), and Arts subjects, where the six forms are subdivided into eight smaller groups.

In September 1989, the Head of the incoming Year Seven was concerned that because of the high proportion of boys to girls, girls would constantly find themselves in a minority situation. Concern had also been expressed over the low GCSE uptake by girls of options traditionally seen as masculine, for example, Technology. Many staff could see that the environment was too often one in which girls were not in a position to participate fully and that boys had more than their fair share of teachers' attention. Some staff thought that the poor attendance of girls might be a result of the gender imbalance.

Bearing in mind research which discusses girls' experiences (Mahony 1989) in mixed groups, the Head of Year, together with the Heads of Science and Maths, requested that the Design Faculty considered the possibility of setting up some single-sex groups for the incoming first year students. For the scheme to go ahead it had to have the support of the Design Faculty as the eight sub-groups operated across Maths, Science and all Design Subjects. The Design Faculty agreed to support this initiative, with the Home Economics Department wholeheartedly in favour and members of both Art and C.D.T. Departments with some reservations. Reservations were, that as a mixed sex, mixed ability school, all groups should be mixed sex and mixed ability and that all-boys groups would be more difficult to teach without the 'calming' influences of the girls. This as we subsequently discovered was an argument used through many decades to support the education of boys at the expense of girls. (Mahony 1985)

Eight groups were set up in September 1989: they consisted of four all-boys, two all-girls and two mixed groups with equal numbers of boys and girls. The tutor groups in this year group were uneven in terms of ability, because all students requiring support had been concentrated into four of the six classes in order to maximise support staff contact time. When tutor groups were subdivided into the eight smaller groups, the belief that high ability girls could cope better with mixed situations was taken into consideration and the two mixed-sex groups comprised entirely of pupils with a reading age above 9.5. The single-sex groups therefore, had a higher concentration of pupils with special educational needs.

During discussions, teachers expressed hopes that they might see some of the following benefits from the new groupings:

- That girls might not always be in minority situations.
- To provide a more supportive environment for girls to develop confidence both in the subject and in themselves.
- To help challenge perceptions of subjects as masculine/ feminine.
- To give girls more access, more teacher time and prevent a group of boys from dominating the lesson.
- To encourage boys to work collaboratively as opposed to competitively.

The staff involved did not see single-sex groupings alone as the answer to solving problems of inequality or under achievement, and realised that many other factors were involved, such as teaching styles, classroom management and the nature of the work set.

The following year (1990), the new intake was organised along the same lines, except there was no policy to place pupils with special needs in any particular group, and therefore, theoretically groups were more even in terms of ability.

The school had an Equal Opportunity Working Party, some of whose members were also part of the Design Faculty Equal Opportunity Group. During discussions over whether to continue the experiment into a second year, concern was expressed that no assessment had been made of how effective the single-sex grouping of the previous year had been. The Equal Opportunity Working Party was concerned that neither parents nor the whole staff had been consulted, or were even aware of single-sex groupings being operated within the school. The children were not aware either of the difference in the groupings because they were new to the school.

Because the Design Faculty Staff were involved in teaching these groups, the Faculty's Equal Opportunity Group was very keen to undertake some monitoring with the involvement of Maths and Science staff, if possible.

1. To analyse the setting arrangements for girls in Year Ten for Maths and Science and their eventual GCSE results.

2. To enable girls to evaluate their own experiences in mixed and single-sex classes by discussion of what would be best for a hypothetical new girl.

3. To produce a staff questionnaire for teachers of all-girls group.

4. To monitor girls' experiences in mixed and single-sex lessons through classroom observation.

The group discussed these plans with Maths and Science staff representatives and they were happy to join the evaluation. Year Eight was targeted for the initial research as the groups had been running longer, and could be expected to be showing more effects.

At this point, in February 1991, we gained the support of the Gender Action Project and our contribution to it became to try and assess the effectiveness of all-girls groups as a strategy to improve the quality of girls' learning and their access to the curriculum. GAP provided us with supply cover so that we could shadow girls over a period of two weeks and with support through regular meetings. As we left the school before these girls chose their GCSE courses, we are unable to present an analysis of subject uptake or exam success in terms of how the groups were organised for Maths, Science, C.D.T. and Home Economics. However, we were able to complete the other three monitoring strategies of the project.

Results 1: Students' Evaluation

Students were told that we were trying to evaluate the different types of groups and they were asked to suggest the best type of group for a new girl arriving at the school. They had to make recommendations based on their own experience, but we felt it would be less threatening for them to discuss another pupil, rather than their own feelings. The following are summaries of pupil discussions.

Girls from girls' groups talking about the benefits of being in a mixed group

'Girls should communicate with both sexes.'

'I would like to hear their opinions.'

'I like some classes with boys because they liven it up and it is boring with all girls.'

'I want to see how the boys work in Science and so I don't have to listen to Ruth's speeches.'

'You can't really compete against girls, boys make it more exciting.'

'We work harder if boys are trying to beat us.'

'We would like to show the boys that they can't do everything better.'

'We should have boys in Home Economics so that we can laugh at them.'

'Home Economics should be mixed so that we can help the boys get high grades.'

'The mixed group is best because the boys can help the girls more.'

'C.D.T. should be mixed so we can take good ideas from the boys.'

'Some boys are good at drawing and you can see their pictures.'

'Boys can do the heavy jobs which some girls aren't strong enough to do.'

'I'd like to be with boys the whole time in C.D.T. because I hate Mr S. and the boys would make us laugh.'

The girls from the all-girls group perceived the benefits of working in a mixed group as providing diversity and competition and being entertained by the boys in the classroom. The girls also felt that they would have welcomed the opportunity to be able to 'learn' from the boys' classwork, and to help the boys with Home Economics, a subject they felt boys would naturally struggle in. What is clear from this is that the girls held fairly stereotyped views about the boys' and girls' 'natural abilities' as being sex differentiated.

Girls from mixed group talking about the benefits of being in a mixed group

'In a mixed group you get more opinions.'

'In a mixed group she can get used to working with both.'

'There's more competition in a mixed group between boys and girls.'

'It might get boring being in an all-girls' group.'

'We think it's more bitchy being in an all-girls' group.'

These girls, like those of the single-sex groups, perceived the benefits as more variety and entertainment. But although some mentioned that it was important to hear different opinions, be in a competitive environment and learn to work with the opposite sex, the majority felt that boys hindered their academic achievement (although not only in the subjects where the single-sex groups existed). It is interesting to note that some thought an all-girls group might be 'bitchy', when girls who had worked in this environment didn't perceive this as a problem.

'We feel we could get more done in a girls' group but we enjoy being in a mixed group so it's balanced.'

'If she can learn in a mixed group we can't see why she can't stay there, but if her grades went down put her in a single-sex group'.

Girls from girls' groups talking about the benefits of single-sex groups

'It's good to be with girls because if you make a mistake they are kinder.'

'You get more done in a girls' group, especially if the work is interesting.'

'You get more concentration and the boys won't disturb us so you can work better.'

'Boys blame things on us. Sometimes the class is noisy and the teachers tell us off for nothing.'

'We get detentions when we are in with the boys, the girls' group never gets one.'

'Girls' group are a break from the boys in case you may be fat or skinny.'

'I like Science with all girls. The lesson is exciting and we have more fun with Miss C.'

'In the girls' group if she spoke a language we can help her.' (from two girls whose first language was not English).

The girls in the single-sex groups discussed the positive benefits of their groupings as getting more work done, getting support, not being harassed by the boys and not getting into trouble.

Girls from mixed groups talking about the benefits of single-sex groups

'We might prefer an all-girls group because in our experience in C.D.T. girls feel intimidated because boys think they are better at that subject than girls.'

'If she wants to learn, go single-sex, if she doesn't, go mixed.'

'In mixed you won't get anywhere, boys mess around a lot.'

'Boys distract more than girls.'

'If you have a problem you can talk about it more with girls rather than boys.'

These girls mentioned the same positive benefits but added, presumably from their own experience of a very male dominated subject, C.D.T., the comment about being undermined. Also, they mention a desire for 'personal space' to talk about things, which they thought would be more possible in an all-girls group.

General

Both girls from single-sex and mixed groups agreed that choice of group depended partly on the girl herself. For instance, 'if she is a quiet girl she might prefer a quiet group where boys won't tease or pick on her. If she is a noisy girl she might prefer a mixed group where she can chat or muck about.'

It would appear from this that girls think confident girls are more able to cope with harassment from boys but less likely to concentrate on the work in a mixed group. Some girls from a mixed group made the point that it depended on the individual boys in their group as well. 'It's better to work with people whose personalities match. The type of boys in our class are different. The other classes have more popular boys – the ones the girls like and the ones that have friends in other years – the ones that are in fashion.'

These girls also seemed to think that in other classes where boys have a high profile as 'boys' rather than 'non-fashionable' fellow students, a girl would have less chance of academic success. A crucial factor for all girls was – 'It depends on which teacher you get' – more about that later.

Finally, one argument in favour of mixed groups for some subjects and single-sex groups for others was 'If the girl came from a mixed school she should experience being in an all-girls group. I think that girls that separate for certain subjects are lucky because they can talk to the girls and have a laugh with the boys and experience both groups. And it's the same for the boys. The girls in this class have to put up with the same boys day in, day out. It gets very boring.'

Results 2: Summary of Staff Feedback

Staff were asked to fill in a questionnaire. They were asked to comment (with specific reference to their subject if possible) on how they felt the gender composition of the all-girls group had affected girls' motivation, achievement, confidence, enjoyment, their own teaching, the content of lessons and anything else they felt to be relevant.

Motivation

All teachers except one felt that the girls in the girls' groups were highly motivated. Several commented that they were more motivated than the all-boys groups. They had a good record of participation in practical tasks, with the exception of one group in Science. One (male) Maths teacher commented that 'some girls do react in an unpredictable manner when a member of the opposite sex enters the class.'

Achievement

Three teachers said quite categorically that the achievement was better in the all-girls groups. One (male) C.D.T. teacher said 'there seems to be more energy generated by the whole group − but I can't say why this is.' 'Lack of disruptive pupils and the listening skills of this particular group are on the whole particularly good.' A (female) Home Economics teacher said that girls were 'more willing to take on board suggestions such as using the library and interviewing other people.' Two (female) teachers mentioned high achievement in collaborative projects and supportive attitudes.

One (male) Art teacher felt his all-girls group achieved less than other groups and tended to go for smaller scale, less ambitious projects than the girls in his mixed group who, he thought, benefitted from the stimulation offered by working alongside boys who were more prepared to be adventurous and experimental in their work. It is interesting to note that this teacher attributed the difference in work to the fact that the group consisted of all girls and did not mention the fact that his mixed group was not only mixed but also of considerably higher ability.

Confidence

The majority of teachers commented that the girls were becoming more assertive.

(Male) C.D.T. teacher: 'They are not afraid to ask questions and can argue points of view persuasively.'

(Female) Home Economics teacher: 'Both girls groups are very assertive and will ask if they require help - more so than my mixed or all-boys group.'

(Female) Home Economics teacher: 'They are more willing to make presentations to the whole group and they work more independently because they are more supportive to each other.'

(Male) Maths teacher: 'Some introverted pupils are gaining more confidence. There is a development of more trust, intimacy and integrity. Seemingly some shy girls are becoming more outgoing and bolder.'

No staff said that all-girls groups had a negative effect on the girls' confidence.

Enjoyment

All staff recorded a high level of enjoyment of lessons apart from one (male) Science teacher who found it varied from lesson to lesson, partly because the girls found it difficult to understand the work. Three teachers commented on better communication between pupils and one (female) teacher said that they showed a great deal of respect and admiration for each other's work.

Teaching styles

General opinions were that less time was spent on discipline and a more relaxed atmosphere was experienced in the class. One all-girls group needed more structured work than the other, due to ability levels. One (male) C.D.T. teacher made conscious efforts to make his subject more 'girl friendly', both in discussion and type of project set. Only one other teacher recorded any difference in her content or approach. Others said courses were too fixed to allow for variations, or that no variation was needed. One (male) Art teacher commented: 'I spend a lot of time being pestered by eyelash fluttering girls asking for help (aren't I lucky!)'.

Content of lessons

Only two teachers had altered the content of their lessons. One (female) teacher commented that girls were more able to determine their own learning activities, because of their co-operative approach.

Other comments

Only four staff recorded comments under this heading.

1. (Female) Home Economics teacher said of the girls' group: 'No group ever dominating, a lot of effort put into homework - better by far than my boys' group. The girls are almost *never* in detention. They come up during the week to do homework or to choose recipes and they clear up without hassle. There is no dumping the clearing up on others, they work co-operatively.'

2. (Male) C.D.T. teacher: 'The group that I taught was exceptionally good - the personalities involved have a lot to do with motivation and levels of attainment. Being an all-girls group might have helped, but I can't say for sure.'

3. (Male) Art teacher. 'Behaviour problems - fewer serious incidents, but a lot of bitchiness and upset.' 'The only noticeable development is an embryonic 'tetchiness' about boys, this intrudes at times.' Given what we know about the effects of teacher expectation on pupil performance and identity, it would be interesting to know to what extent this teacher's own perceptions of girls 'intruded' in their progress.

Classroom monitoring

This was carried out by two different (female) teachers using monitoring sheets of the same design.

All types of group responded to different individual teachers in different ways. Pupils' perceptions, teachers' organisation, their style and experience, affected pupils' attitudes and behaviour. In mixed groups the girls sat together in blocks so conversation with other girls was possible in both types of group. When pupils were clear about the task and work was appropriate, girls remained on task for 90 per cent of the time in all-girls situations, but only 60 per cent of the time in mixed situations as boys took up more teacher time, interfered with girls' work and dominated use of equipment.

Teachers were aware of our focus and so may have been more aware of their own practice in relation to equal opportunities. Over half the teachers we observed teaching mixed groups spoke to us about their concern to give girls equal access and boost their confidence in the mixed situation and, with one (male) exception, girls were asked as many class questions as boys, with all teachers (male and female) carefully avoiding situations where girls were likely to be ridiculed.

In the all-girls groups there was generally more verbal negotiation with the teacher, each other, and us as observers, with the girls showing a lot of interest in what we were doing. A wider range of girls were prepared to put their hand up and answer a question, not just the very confident ones.

In the all-girls groups in practical lessons the verbal negotiations included discussion and comparison of work, with girls showing interest in the achievement of others and offering support and helpful advice. In the all-girls groups, girls benefitted from more hands-on experience of tools, equipment and computers with 'turns' being negotiated rather than competed for. Tasks were therefore completed faster, providing a more encouraging experience. At the end of some lessons the girls in all-girls groups were reluctant to clear up and wanted to continue with the work whereas in mixed classes they packed away immediately when asked.

In the mixed groups, boys had to be corrected for behaviour more than three times as often as girls. It was also noticed that particular characters tended to dominate in the mixed groups, (again, usually boys), whereas in the all-girls groups teacher attention was more likely to be evenly spread between pupils.

In the single sex groups the 'bad' behaviour of some girls became higher profile, although generally less time was spent on discipline and more on the subject of the lesson. This 'bad behaviour' was particularly noticeable when male teachers were teaching the all-girls groups. Interestingly, (whether accidentally or because all-girl groups were thought to present fewer discipline problems), departments did not assign any 'high profile authoritarian' male teachers to these groups. The quieter, less 'macho' males that taught them definitely suffered more discipline problems than the female staff, throughout the subject range.

Conclusion

Those of us involved in the monitoring of the success of single-sex groups as a strategy for improving girls' achievement and access, found the girls' groups to have been to some extent, successful. Considerable evidence was generated which shows that in terms of confidence, girls benefitted from their time in single-sex groups, although we are not able to say whether their improved confidence stayed with them on their return to a mixed situation.

As a result of our project we would make the following recommendations.

1. Single-sex groups should be a whole school initiative preceded by thorough staff discussion. Management support is essential and monitoring time should be built into the school's meeting programme so that it does not disappear down to the bottom of a list of priorities. All staff, including supply and cover teachers could be involved in the monitoring.

    In our case we encountered problems because we inherited a situation where the opinion of the whole school was not canvassed and not all staff were in favour. Some staff were even unaware that single-sex groups existed. The intended liaison between Science, Maths and Design broke down due to pressure of work. Had it not been for the Design Faculty who had undertaken the monitoring we might have found it impossible to complete the task.

    Our experience has been that if teachers have ownership of any initiative implemented in their school, they will try hard to make it work. In our school, more ownership might have led to all staff taking a more serious approach to the project and addressing gender issues inherent in their own practice. Also, parents and pupils should have been involved from the beginning of the project. When staff discussed the type of group that the child was in as part of feedback to parents at Parents' Evening, no one recorded any objections from parents. One mother expressed wholehearted approval of the idea, saying that it would give her daughter 'the best of both worlds', whilst the father said he did not see any difference between the opportunities offered in either type of group.

2. An experiment such as this should be part of a schools' development plan. It could, as in the case of Reed House, be part of staff development on Equal Opportunity. For example, working together to establish priorities for monitoring would make staff examine their own attitudes and practice. This would also give such an initiative a definite time scale and build in public performance indicators.

3. As many variables as possible need to be eliminated for instance, single-sex and mixed 'control' groups should be of equal ability as far as possible. Factors such as the gender of the teacher, size of the class, nature of the subject and layout of the room, need to be taken into consideration. It would be helpful if pupils could be observed studying the same subject in different types of groups. In our own attempts to monitor, it was difficult to compare, for example, the performance of the same girl in a mixed-sex Humanities class with her performance in a single-sex Science class. It would also have been revealing to watch the same girl with the same teacher in a mixed-sex Science lesson and a single-sex Science lesson.

4. While Home Economics and C.D.T. have been traditionally sex stereotypical areas and there has been evidence to show that girls' experiences in Maths and Science are different to boys, as far as we know Art is not a subject where girls are marginalised to the same extent at school. We would therefore, recommend that the focus for further work should be Technology, Science and Maths.

In our own school we encountered a wide variety of staff attitudes to gender equality. In looking at the total experience of a few girls over a week it transpired that some girls were taught by female teachers for over three quarters of their time in school and others by male teachers for over three quarters of their timetable. It also became apparent that male staff were more likely to experience disruptive problems with some girls' groups than female staff. We found ourselves increasingly of the opinion that the gender and attitude of the teacher are among the most important factors in influencing pupil attitudes and behaviour. This is an area which is in urgent need of further research (and, of course, *action)*.

Introducing the School in which the projects described in chapters four to six were undertaken

The area around Netley Primary School consists mostly of streets of terraced Victorian houses, either owner-occupied or rented. The majority of pupils (about 85 per cent) are Muslim, from families who began to settle in the area in the 1960s, arriving from the Asian peninsula and other Commonwealth countries. Most pupils are accomplished bilingual speakers, although there is always a small proportion of beginner bilingual children in the school at any one time. The school usually has additional support from a Section 11 teacher (funded directly by the government to support children whose first language is not English). The school is a one-form entry primary school offering just over two hundred places. It is housed in an old Victorian building with a very small asphalt playground which has been extended since the time of the project. During the project, there were eight classes taught by seven full-time teachers (including the deputy headteacher) and two teachers working in a job-share. In addition on the staff were the headteacher and a part-time reading and language support teacher.

If this project demonstrates anything, it shows how complex an initiative can become once it starts to grow within a gender-friendly environment. Our project became a many-headed beast, a chimera. Writing about it is equally complicated and could not realistically take the form of a description of what we did in the order in which it happened. Nor is the story finished. We still have a long way to go before the issues we have raised are even part-way resolved.

There were four main reasons for becoming involved in the project. One was that other staff in the school were interested and offering to join in. The second was that we had a sympathetic and effective acting headteacher who went out of his way to support us. The third reason was that the project carried with it some resources, and we felt strongly that any available resources should be pulled into the school. The fourth reason was because I had had an idea which I wanted to try out: I knew from my own biography that observation is a powerful tool for raising awareness and I wanted to find out whether it would be an effective strategy to get *the pupils* undertaking observation and research.

The news that the school would be given eight days cover for the project seemed incredible, but it also made us think that it seemed grossly unfair for all the resources to go to one teacher. It was at this point that we began to see the project as something which ought to take a higher profile within the school rather than an idea which one or two teachers were interested in. Somehow the degree of resourcing available made us determined to think on a larger scale. I really do not believe that this was due to the money so much as a realisation that people were depending on us to do what we had said we would do, and were prepared to back our efforts to a degree so far unknown in our careers or in the history of the school.

Pat Mahony came into the school before any work on the project began. I cannot stress enough how important this was in basing the project firmly within the school rather than within one individual's involvement. A small primary school does not receive many visitors. So a visit from someone outside the education authority, coming to talk about something which was an innovation in the school, was a powerful statement to all the staff that this project mattered, and the school mattered.

Many teachers in our careers in schools have experiences where new ideas were blocked, undermined, or sabotaged by those with the power to do that. On the other side many of us have also worked in contexts where we have felt nurtured, valued and empowered. This project was of the latter variety, and the final product is surely evidence of the success of a management style on the part of the school and the local authority which produces that effect.

In the following three chapters we describe some of the work we did: the work with staff is described in chapter four, our work with children as researchers is the subject of chapter five and finally in chapter six we describe the way in which we used the National Curriculum to support our gender work.

CHAPTER FOUR

Putting Gender on the Agenda

Marjorie Smith

Our decision to interview all the teaching staff in the school about their perceptions of gender issues arose from a number of factors. Firstly, the fact that we had some funding to undertake the project meant that this mammoth task would actually be possible. Supply cover was available to ensure that the interviews could take place within school time.

Secondly, and more importantly, there was the perceived need to produce a gender policy for the school. So often policies are written in the absence of any prior, concurrent (or even subsequent?) change in practice. Even worse, individual teachers try out new ideas and make important new discoveries without having any impact at all on the policies of the school or its practice. We intended, where possible, to utilise our findings when setting up the project with Class 6, and also to feed back our collective experience and knowledge to the discussions about a gender policy. Interviewing the staff was seen as a good first start to encouraging discussion and for helping us to gauge what the focus of further work should be with the staff as a whole.

Rather than just using the teachers as a resource for interview material, we wanted to provide some input as well. Two of us gathered a set of selected readings together and made a booklet of them called 'Gender Action'. All the staff had easy access to the reading material and everyone was given supply cover for an hour, to give them some reading time. Although this took up two days of our supply cover for the project, I felt it was well worth it. The reading itself took far more than an hour, but most people read all the readings, and everyone read some. Staff really appreciated being given time for this purpose, even though it was inadequate.

The interviews were conducted in the week following the launch of the 'Gender Action' booklet and the teachers' reading time. We hoped that the readings would help staff to focus on the issues and therefore identify factors for our consideration more effectively.

I conducted all the interviews within one day while a supply teacher moved from class to class to cover each teacher. Ten teachers were interviewed. Of these, all were white of British origin, and eight were women. (The gender and race imbalances here are, sadly, not unusual). Length of teaching experience in primary schools ranged from three years to over thirty years, with the exception of one probationary teacher. Eight had taught in other schools prior to working at this school. Seven of the interviewees were class teachers, three currently teaching infant classes and four currently teaching junior classes. Within the past year, five of the interviewees had taught both infants and juniors within the school. One of the class teachers was from the borough 'unattached' service, temporarily covering for the long-term absence of the headteacher. Of the others, one had a part-time post, one was a member of the Multicultural Development Service and one was acting headteacher.

The class teachers (working in a job-share) of the top infant class were not included in the interviews because the first run of Standard Assessment Tests was going through at that time.

All the interviewees had earlier been given a short written description to explain the purpose of the interviews and the intentions of the project. Questions were not given in advance, but written questions were provided at the time of the interview for reference purposes. Responses were tape-recorded and subsequently transcribed. The questions were as follows:

1. What gender issues concern you in your class this year?

2. Have you tried to tackle any of these problems?
    If so, what did you do and what happened?

3. What gender issues concern you throughout the school:
    (a) pupils
    (b) staff
    (c) parents
    (d) other?

4. Do you think we could do more in classrooms to combat inequalities between the sexes?

5. Are there any other ways in which you think we could effectively foster equal opportunities in school?

6. With respect to the project, are there any areas in school where you think further observation would be informative?

7. Are there any ways in which you think the school differs from others in respect to gender?

8. What gender issues concern you within the wider community around the school?

9. Have you any observations to make on gender issues within Class 6?

10. Have the readings helped you to focus on the issue of gender? Were any particularly helpful/not helpful?

The results of the interviews have not been grouped as responses to individual questions. Other issues clearly emerged as important, and it seemed more profitable to organise answers according to the patterns dictated by teachers' concerns. Individual teachers have not been identified, but if the teacher is referring only to infants or juniors, rather than the primary age range, then this is noted.

Shortly after the interviews took place, we arranged a short staff meeting to discuss the issues within a larger group. Many of the points which emerged in the interviews were reiterated, and so these are reported here also.

In retrospect, I might well not have asked specific questions at all, but simply requested interviewees to talk about gender issues within the school. Overall, there was a marked consistency across all the interviewees, and priorities and concerns were generally very similar. One major theme which emerged was the strength of the school in relation to gender. On reflection, the above questions are all rather negative, and no question was specifically asked about the school's successes. Even so, several staff referred to the general level of awareness of gender issues amongst the teaching staff in very positive terms:

> T: I think people are aware and working on it, certainly the staff are ... but I think some of the pupils are not yet convinced ... namely boys.

The fact that the project was taking place in a school which, in staff terms at least, was beyond the level of elementary consciousness-raising was an important point in determining the project's potential. Without exception, all teachers who were interviewed considered themselves to be responding to gender considerations in some way and to some degree. Without exception, all teachers saw this as important and necessary. These factors permitted us to seek a direction for positive, pro-active work in the field of gender.

It could be argued that the readings 'primed' acceptable responses from teachers, but I am convinced that this was not the case. The more recently recruited teachers in the school had, in any case, covered aspects of gender in education as part of their studies:

> T: They definitely did help me focus, got me fired up again which was really good. I mean, some of them were not helpful in the sense that I'd read them before, but I quite enjoyed reading it all again.

Many staff in the school, including some who had left and were therefore not interviewed, have a long-term and abiding interest in gender issues. The effect that these people have had on the school is a very important one:

> T: ... So many of (the readings) reminded me of things that Ann and Jean (teachers who have since left) had already said in the staffroom...

There was also some evidence of staff appointments having been being affected by a commitment to gender:

> T: There has been a tremendous amount of change amongst the staff over the years. There was tremendous antipathy, enormous feeling against change, in lining up, de-sectioning of registers ... and to look back at that and the way staff talk about these things now ... I think that has been very much down to [the headteacher at that time] in terms of the sort of thing he was looking for when he was appointing staff.

Many staff recognised the fact that the staffing hierarchy itself invited sexist assumptions from the pupils:

> T: ... and the messages that we give to children, for example, a male head of a school — there must be some message there.

For years the school had employed male headteachers and deputy headteachers, and the male deputy headteacher had taken the 'top' Year 6 class for some time. One or two staff voiced hopes that there would be a woman headteacher or deputy headteacher in the near future, and, hopefully, a male teacher in the infant department.

One major criticism of staff emerged, identified by one teacher:

> T: I think what bothered me most was that boys were allowed to get away with things and that's something I really did notice. When boys are naughty, oh well, that's just a boy being naughty. Whereas when a girl's naughty that's classed as quite bad and it's pulled up

on much more that it is with a boy. That seems to me to be very unfair and unjust. (Juniors).

Another theme which emerged from the interviews was the different ways in which teachers understood and responded to gender. All staff identified 'gender problems' within their own classrooms and within the school environment, but one of the most striking factors which emerged was that the majority of staff were identifying only those problems which might be categorised as 'management' issues. 'Management' issues are so-called here because they are perceived as related to inappropriate behaviour. The type of behaviour regularly mentioned constitutes an all-too-familiar list (Weiner, 1990).

Boys' domination of space was a major concern, particularly outside the classroom itself:

T: ...general dominance of the boys in the playground and moving about the building. Their games tend to be far more spread out than the girls', and the girls' activities are peripheral.

T: I think lining up and coming in for lunch - who sits at which table for lunch. There's often this business about saving seats and ... it's generally the girls who move to a different table if the boys come.

Many recognised the differential amounts of time and attention received by the two sexes as problematic:

T: In most classes boys do get more share of the teacher attention but I think that's because they behave in a way whereby they demand more attention and girls don't. Boys get a larger share of teacher attention and to a certain extent of space as well. Because of the way they sit and their physical qualities as well, they just seem to demand a greater share of the cake in almost everything.

T: ...I came out (of the class) thinking; 'I've seen about five or six faces', and they were all boys and even if it was going quite nicely they would do something silly just to stop it, for attention, showing off, basically.

Access to equipment was also mentioned:

T: As regards the boys pushing the girls away from certain activities, it does still go on unless it is constantly watched because the girls will give way. Construction toys – the girls will play with a group of girls, they will actually use the equipment, but I haven't managed to get mixed groups using it. If any boys join the group, they take over and the girls think it's perfectly all right for the boys to take over... (Infants).

Fourthly, boys taking control of activities:

T: Well I have done it in drama and PE, doing group work ... I let them choose their own groups and devise their own games with PE equipment. Then I made three from each group move around, so that in the end they were mixing with children they wouldn't normally mix with. And I watched, and nine times out of ten it was the boys deciding the rules of the game. I mean, you wouldn't let that happen normally, but that's what it looked like from a distance. (Juniors).

Finally, boys failing to do tidying jobs and girls doing tidying jobs for them:

T: You often see things being pushed across the table for someone else to clear up. Is it just anybody doing that or is it just boys for the girls to clear up? Roles that they take upon themselves within the classroom ... I mean you and I can say 'clear up' but they take up the roles that they see for themselves already.

One teacher felt that problems with infants were not significant.

T: I haven't noticed any real gender issues ... At infant level there isn't much difference. As they get to junior level they begin to develop differently. (Infants).

Others, however, had noticed quite marked differences.

T: Mainly the boys being rather dominant and there are more boys than girls and the boys are generally bigger, noisier, more assertive than the girls. The girls can quite easily finish up rather underfoot. (Infants).

The above fairly typical examples were not seen as due to the inappropriate behaviour of boys alone. Quite clearly, the 'passive' and more amenable nature of the girls was also perceived as a factor in permitting the rise of these unequal situations.

From all staff, however, there was the clear understanding that boys' domination and control was unacceptable, and that solutions must be sought:

T: Unless we are really vigilant, and make sure that we follow up and we're on the ball with it, it just becomes part of the school's hidden curriculum, that the children accept, and I think it's very unfair - they can't fight that on their own, they need the support that everybody's reacting the same towards it.

Staff described a number of strategies which they used to combat the difficulties they encountered.

Sometimes, although rarely, it was a matter of discipline:

> T: ...and stamping on language that's used out in the playground as heavily as swearing, like 'dog' and 'slut'. (Juniors).

Careful observation and monitoring were mentioned by a number of teachers. Sometimes this was straightforward vigilance:

> T: Constant monitoring to ensure that girls do get a fair chance at everything and that the boys don't push the girls out of certain areas and equally leave certain areas to the girls, like cleaning up which most of the boys are very reluctant to do, and will find a girl to do if not watched. That's very much improved with a lot of nagging and not letting a boy just sit on the carpet and send a girl to do it. (Infants).

Observation was also perceived, however, as a means of identifying the areas which we needed to be working on:

> T: ... catch what they're saying and then you know how you're going to have to educate them.

Self-monitoring by staff would also come into this category, but, although it was mentioned, no-one reported that they undertook to self-monitor on any regular basis.

Several staff gave examples which showed that they were combatting problems by organising the classroom in a more enlightened way:

> T: At the beginning of the year, first of all, whenever I noticed that certain boys weren't actually involved with tidying up then we all sat down except for those boys and they actually did the tidying up and I had other children of both sexes showing them where things went, teaching them. And whenever I chose people to do jobs, I would choose the opposite to the way they expected, that is the boys to wash up and girls to move furniture. Or mixed groups, I mean I tended to go more for mixed groups, partners, to do jobs. (Infants).

Another response to management problems which one or two staff were clearly in the habit of utilising was positive action, whereby girls are deliberately given additional or special access to time and attention, as a means of counteracting the more usual patterns which occur in classrooms.

> T: I'll find time for the girls at dinner time or after school. They all stay, and then I'll give them that sort of positive extra input into what they're doing and how well they can do it. I do it during class as well, but somehow that's all a bit ad hoc.
> T: I've always tried to see through the boys anyway, and to see the girls,

and to bring them out with questions and say: 'That's a good answer', and so on.

Similarly, positive action was used in the allocation of resources:

> T: Within the classroom, perhaps with Design and Technology, if the girls are given a box of brand new Lego first and given a task and left to get on with it, it would give them more attention and more prestige. Often the boys make a dive for it and the girls, whether they want to or not, they should be given the chance. And it's often that they just lack confidence with it because so often girls are brought up with girls' toys, and the boys get the building things, the Lego. So I think it's just confidence with the materials that they're using.

Using positive action is not without its difficulties. The following quote from a teacher who regularly uses positive action in her classroom exemplifies the kind of complex decisions which teachers have to make several times a day, that balance between ensuring access and acceding to reasonable requests.

> T: I've watched for grabbing equipment first. What concerns me really is how much time I give to boys because I think I'm reacting to them differently and I think it's because they're more demanding and they always request the computer or the 'Roamer' much more than the girls and really it's because they're asking they end up having it and girls always see them on it. To combat it I always try and give to the girls first. But at the same time I don't want to say no to these boys who want to have a go at it. (Juniors).

The same teacher was well aware of the problems which can arise when using positive action.

> T: It's really strange because the boys will complain if they think the girls are being chosen too much. They say it's always girls that are being chosen – well it is, but it's also that they are so much more demanding. Actually if it's boys all the time the girls very rarely complain.

Whilst there are clear indications that staff had a variety of responses at their disposal, there is also a strong suggestion in these responses that teachers utilised these methods of ensuring 'fair play' without necessarily explaining their reasoning to the pupils concerned:

> T: There are certain things like the lining up. I would always choose people to line up by doing mental arithmetic and things so that way they would line up rather than it always being the boys to push, but they weren't aware that I was organising it. (Infants).

This raises a fascinating question. Is it enough to ensure that girls have equal access to attention, space and resources? A skilled teacher could undertake to do this without ever openly declaring her motives to the pupils. Ensuring equal access would certainly be an achievement, and would give girls a fairer deal within the classroom, but in the longer term this would not effect a raising of pupils' awareness. Girls could leave an environment relatively unskilled in dealing with boys' behaviour because they are continually shielded from it. Boys would not be confronted with the reasons why teachers make certain decisions. One teacher made this point, raising alongside it the difficulties of finding appropriate language.

> T: We could talk to the children about it, explain that we are trying not to be sexist. I don't know what language we could use, we would have to be a bit careful on that. (Infants).

As part of the project with Class 6, we attempted to articulate the problems with the pupils, to make quite explicit our motivations and intentions. Part of this exercise would include the exploration of appropriate and effective language. We were aware that there were problems of appropriate language, even with junior pupils:

> T: The juniors are aware of the terms 'sexism' and 'racism', but I don't think they really understand sexism. They think it means either working with boys or girls or not. They don't really understand the wider issues at all.

Yet most children, even at reception level, recognise the concept of 'fairness':

> T: I've heard girls saying; 'Oh it's not fair, when I get home I have to look after my brothers and sisters and my big brother can watch television but I've got to help mum.'

It was through the concepts of fairness that we decided to approach the work with Class 6. The Anti-Sexist Working Party (1985) had found this to be a successful approach in their work:

> We have found that children have a strong sense of fairness and justice and when given encouragement to make their own decisions are quick to challenge inequality.

The next stage would then be to ask pupils to make their own observations and judgements and come up with their own suggestions. Pupils might, for example, find out for themselves that boys use the computer or the 'Roamer' more, and might even put forward some solutions. We hoped that the project with Class 6 might provide some of the answers.

However, there was evidence that articulating the problems, raising the issues with pupils could create unwanted side-effects.

T: Once you start explaining and showing these behaviour patterns — it's the same with bullying — any bullying talk I do there's a spate of it afterwards, and I don't know why it is, it must be the way I'm saying it. Or the fact that I'm bringing it up and now they all come and tell me. It's all been going on and now I've actually addressed it.

I: So you think there might be a knock-on effect of trying to tackle gender in any class?

T: Because I've seen boys going 'Yeah, Yeah' and start seeing it as a boys versus girls thing.

It may indeed be experiences of this kind which lead teachers not to clarify their motives. Also a recognition of something else:

T: But it's not a solution, it's just that in trying to tackle these things you've just thrown up the problem. You set yourself up by creating these situations.

All the teachers interviewed recognised at least some of the imbalances in their classrooms, and all were attempting to address those factors which they perceived. A much smaller group (less than half) recognised the need to develop a wider perspective on gender, which I will refer to as 'curriculum' issues. Whereas 'management' issues refer to the behaviour of the pupils and the ways in which teachers respond to this, 'curriculum' issues here refer to what we teach, how we teach and the materials we use. I have deliberately avoided the use of the term 'hidden curriculum' in this context. There are, of course, aspects of both management and curriculum issues which contribute to the hidden curriculum.

A number of areas were identified. One of them was that of visitors to the school. There is currently no policy relating to visitors to the school, but clearly gender should be a factor in determining selection of appropriate visitors or speakers.

T: Getting into the school some role models, people who have broken the mould, who are doing what was previously considered to be a male thing. We should fall over backwards — and would probably have to — to find women who could fit that, but I'm sure that we could, actually. When you pass building sites you see women with hard hats on. I think we could really say could you come to our school and talk to the children, maybe try and get in touch with some really high-powered business women to come and talk and say: 'I've done it'. I think that sort of thing makes a big impression on children, I think they remember that kind of thing.

The need to address gender through role models in relation to race and disability was another factor.

> T: I also think we could get more outside speakers in who are good role models for the children ... especially women from the ethnic minorities.

> T: Disabled people as well, show it can be done. We have had a disabled woman in school − she's made it.

So often race, gender and disability are considered as separate entities and only recently have we begun to look more closely at the implications of that. We must recognise the limitations of white women as role models to Asian and Afro-Caribbean girls. It is also important to recognise the implications of religion and culture in determining girls' aspirations and futures. One of the factors which we have now begun to consider in this school is the importance of inviting speakers who are Muslim women and who wear the traditional shalwar kameez of the children's local community.

The same, of course, applies to visual aids showing women's achievements.

> T: I think there should be more posters and more things around showing women in top jobs, more posters, more books, there's not a lot of resources around.

There was clearly a lot of emphasis placed on the importance of providing career models, as opposed to positive images. This seemed to be the main purpose attributed to visitors, posters, and so on in relation to gender. This poses the question as to whether the process of encouraging girls to aspire to a wider range of careers is achieved only by providing role models and posters. We need to recognise that, for the majority of women, a demanding career will mean having to deal with competing responsibilities and duties, competition from men, and, at times, disapproval from colleagues and/or family. It is therefore important to ensure that, whilst we raise expectations, we also encourage the development of the awareness, skills and courage which girls and young women will inevitably need if they are to 'break the mould'.

However, if women need awareness and skills to deal with their career decisions, do they not also, just as much, need the wherewithal, the 'life skills', to deal with school? Take, for example, the situation described in the following interview and consider just how much there is within it for all the girls and all the boys to learn about themselves.

> T: And there are some boys in that class who are very quiet and gentle but they're not the leaders in the class. It's almost a way of developing them as well so that they're − I think that the children in there are very threatened. It's harder to get to the bottom of who they're threatened by, it's about four individuals, really... They are very aggressive and very mocking and that permeates the whole class and no-one dares say anything because they don't want to be laughed at.
>
> I: If those four individuals were girls do you think the problems would be the same?
>
> T: I think we're looking at sexism. The way those individuals react is in a very male stereotyped way. Also the way the girls have retreated back from them. There are some girls who get on all right because they're popular, because they fit the kind of criteria that's needed. There's just no space for individuals in there − it's really quite horrible.
>
> I: And do you think the popular girls are falling into a particular role?
>
> T: Yes. Definitely. They're either becoming loud and flirtatious or they're absolutely retreating back and not saying anything about anybody and being accepted for just being quiet and passive. No. They're not standing up just for themselves to be as they want to be.

The uncomfortable truth may be that we do not know how to handle some of these situations effectively. We have to question seriously whether we distance ourselves from these complex (and unpleasant) realities by concerning ourselves with the children's future existences more than with their present lives.

Those staff who approached gender as a 'curriculum' issue highlighted the need for appropriate teaching materials:

> T: Books, for example. Important to ensure first of all that there are enough books portraying women in a positive and strong light and then to make sure once you had those books, which I don't think most schools do have enough of because they're not produced anyway, to then ensure that the children read them and that work could be done on them. I think there aren't enough.

It was these teachers who recognised the need to make women, girls' and women's concerns much more explicit within the curriculum. In their efforts to do this, they have, of course, come up against the extraordinary dearth of information and back up materials, which is

exacerbated within our own school as no doubt in many others, by the
unavailability of funds to purchase what is available.

> T: I think we could have a good look at our teaching materials, topic
> books, worksheets available. I mean I'm doing the development of
> transport at the moment and it's really hard to find information on
> the women's role apart from Amy Johnson... We did find some-
> thing out about highwaywomen, but it took an awful lot of time, it
> isn't readily available. A lot of materials we've got are just so old.
> That's really it. We've got a lot of really old books and old
> materials. (Juniors).

Some material is available on loan from local resources, and obviously
every possible advantage should be taken of these facilities, but there is
clearly a major issue here for any school which attempts to include
gender as part of the curriculum. Those staff who were consciously
including gender in their teaching were hindered in their work by a
general lack of information, teaching materials and resources.

Three teachers specifically mentioned gender as something they
would deliberately attempt to cover as part of every topic.

> T: We were talking in Kathy's class about Bessie Coleman the first
> black woman pilot. Kathy's very good at drama anyway, and the
> children are very aware now that she was a woman and a black
> woman, who in spite of those things and the prejudice she
> encountered, she triumphed.

In looking at how we might encourage the spread of more 'curriculum'
gender work, it should be noted that the staff concerned were all
referring to work they were undertaking with junior classes at the time.
There could have been a number of reasons for this. There was the
possibility that teachers felt that infants were too young to understand
the issues, although the requirement to 'manage' the classroom in
gender terms was still there.

> T: I think with infants it's more things like making sure that the boys
> do take their turns at clearing up...and it's just making sure that
> the organisation and structure ensure that they actually take equal
> turns.

Choice of topics is certainly a factor which must affect the potential of
topic-based gender work. In her article 'Dinosaurs in the Classroom'
Clarricoates (1987) argues that primary schools select topics which are
more accessible to boys than to girls. There are a number of reasons why
this may be the case. One is that boys will simply not engage in what they
see as a girls' activity or a girls' role.

T: The other thing in drama is when you take on various roles and try to bring in positive images of women, and I take on a man's role and I take on a woman's role. And when I ask the children to do that they will readily take on male roles, but the boys won't readily take on women's roles. The girls will take on male roles without any question, it won't cause too much fuss. But you try to get the boys to take on female roles and they devise all sorts of ways of getting out of it, like: 'Yeah, well, the family I belong to has got an elder brother...' and another one was: 'Well I've just come along to watch the women do these things...' Just devising ways of getting out of it because they can't. They have great difficulty and they're not even being nasty about it. It's just: 'I can't be a girl'. (Juniors)

In Netley Primary, at the time of the project, topics were predetermined for the first half of a term, whilst teachers had free choice for the second half. Initial scrutiny of the topic plan might well indicate a bias in favour of 'male' topics, but one reason for this could be the influence of the National Curriculum for Science, which was the first document to be introduced. Kelly (1987) argues that science is constructed as 'masculine' within schools, both in the way it is presented (the use of examples and so on) and in the classroom interactions which take place during science work. The behaviour of boys, already described here, actually assists their progress in a science learning context. As science assumes a higher status (that is, as part of the core curriculum), there is the danger that girls will become increasingly marginalised. It may well be necessary to look carefully at the methods and examples used in teaching 'masculine' subjects like Science and Design and Technology.

We also have to be careful that we do not devalue the activities and interests which traditionally fall into the 'girls' domain. There is certainly evidence that boys do this:

T: The other thing is the feeling of anything traditionally feminine being inferior, such as football, the feeling it's a boy's game and girls are 'allowed' to play — it's this business of 'allowing'. But you do it the other way round, with 'in and out the dusty windows' (a playground game) or whatever and the boys won't join in on them at all. And if they did there would be pressure from other boys, and even though there are some boys who would like to mix and who would play these games quite happily, they are under a lot of pressure from the others who feel it's somehow 'cissy'.

Whilst boys might be criticised for doing this, it is important to ensure that schools are not guilty of a similar misdemeanour. Often this arises from an attempt to discourage girls from adopting stereotypical interests, or out of concern not to make girls feel that they are only valued for the way they look. Teachers in particular may have difficulties with girls' interests which they perceive as interfering with our objectives of encouraging girls to be independent, active and assertive learners. One teacher describes this very candidly:

> T: What shows up most is the girls tend to be very feminine. They greet me and show me their dresses. That does concern me in terms of how much emphasis I should put on it, and how much to ignore it and try and point to other things that aren't so feminine. We have sharing time every morning and the girls bring in teddy bears and dolls and show the things they are wearing that day. Whereas the boys don't do that at all. They bring in calculators, keyrings, helmets and bulldog clips. This is just so noticeable...That's one of the things that concerns me is how much I should interfere in this. I try to show an interest in something other than teddies and dolls although I do have to recognise that they've brought something in that they want to show and they like. We do get over it a bit by asking them to design some clothes for the bear, so they don't just play 'mummies and daddies'. (Infants).

The teachers who recognised gender as a 'curriculum' issue were also those who recognised the need for progression and continuity for gender teaching within the school.

> T. But I don't know if that will be an ongoing thing, will the next class teacher do it, because we haven't got a policy on it. To make sure that we do it.
>
> T: It should be part of a grand plan, not an accident.

This is a strong argument in favour of a gender policy, or even a gender curriculum. An essential component of this will have to be the issue of evaluation:

> T: ... and how do we know we're getting it right?

This issue is taken up again in Chapter 6.

As well as the many aspects of gender education which teachers did identify, it is important also to highlight those aspects of the curriculum which were not indicated by staff. If curriculum issues refer to what we teach and the materials we use, then there are several other aspects to this which did not emerge through the interview process. We have not, for example, considered whether teachers have different expectations of boys and girls. There are also issues relating to the teaching methods we use, the records we keep, and the methods of assessment we undertake, which remain so far unexplored.

A very strong theme which emerged through answers rather than being elicited through questions was the concern and anxieties teachers had about their own competence to deal with gender issues, and the shifting ground in relation to their own inevitable sexism.

> T: I think it needs another person to come into the room and see what's going on. I don't mean to be sexist but it's the way I was brought up. Often things come out and we don't really want them to come out that way. You know you've said the wrong thing and done the wrong thing. And sometimes you don't know, or even you haven't said something that you should have. And sometimes you need somebody else to see these things going on and point them out. (A woman teacher).

> T: The problem I would find with myself would be because things happen at such a rate, at such times you are obviously off guard. As a man I find I challenge myself about this, but when fifteen things are happening at once, your upbringing. . . I like to think I'm aware of the issues, but there are times, when the pressure's on, when you're off guard.

Some staff wanted more direction and guidance

> T: I'd like to think (we could do more), but as to what. . . I keep trying things but it's a bit like painting the Forth Bridge. I don't know but I don't believe that it's not possible, it's just how to be most effective.

Others recognised the need for more discussion and reflection as a staff:

> T: I think a good way forward is for the staff to have a look at what we mean by sexism and, within this policy of equality, to work out what we mean by 'discrimination', what do we mean by 'gender'. Because everyone will say we all want equality within the pupils but do we actually do it? I mean practically how much does that really happen, and how much do we think we're doing OK but we're actually not? Some of the things we say, and all our inborn sexism.

The uncertainties reflected here argue for a system of supporting staff in their efforts to develop their own thinking and practice in relation to gender. Phrases used like being 'off-guard', knowing you've done or said the 'wrong thing', suggest a degree of anxiety about the whole matter which could easily become counter-productive unless guidance is offered in a safe, non-threatening environment.

Not all the adults working in the school are teachers, although only teachers were interviewed on this occasion. The teachers' views were quite clear that any policy should encompass all staff and visitors.

> T: There are and there always have been a few staff here who are very concerned with issues of gender but by the same token there are

people who are working equally closely with the children who haven't ever had to consider that, such as ancillary staff. And perhaps if we worked towards a policy that includes all people... because obviously kids are getting a totally different message.

It was felt that mid-day assistants in particular, experienced difficulties.

> T: The boys get away with a great deal more in terms of bad table manners and being rude to dinner ladies. The dinner ladies accept rudeness from boys in a way that they don't from girls.

The suggested solution:

> T: ...yet more training sessions. I think the gender issue could be included in the training sessions they have.

A factor which cannot be ignored here is that all the dinner assistants are women, and the pupils can hardly fail to recognise the inevitable school hierarchy which puts teachers at the 'top' and leaves other people near or at the bottom. It is much harder to elicit reasonable behaviour from pupils who perceive you to be of low status, as many teachers, particularly women teachers, already know. This is part of a much wider problem to do with how boys (and perhaps girls, too) perceive women, outside of the exceptional power relationships within the classroom, and any action should certainly attempt to address the wider issue through work with pupils as much as with adults.

All staff were of the view that it would be beneficial to involve parents in work on gender.

> T: Look at it in the very long term and hope that when children who are at school now become parents the problems will be less, but I do see it being an incredibly long-term struggle but every generation will move it a little way and a little bit further.

This was not perceived to be an easy task. Parents, after all, reflect the views of society in general (as do teachers), and represent a whole variety of perspectives:

> T: Some existing parents, yes, you can convince, but others you could lose very fast. They'll pay lip-service to it. I've come across it more than once where parents if you actually speak to them concerning either gender or race, yes, they'll agree with you but in actual fact don't change their behaviour. And I don't know how you tackle that. I don't think you can. You just keep trying. And hope eventually something will come.

There was a recognition that we needed first to determine what parents views actually are on the matter, and also to educate parents as to the rationale behind the school's aims:

> T: It would be really interesting to have an open evening with parents like those curriculum evenings where it's discussed, because if you talked about it in terms of fairness − equal opportunities to education − most parents want the best for their children, be they girls or boys, and aren't going to want their children to suffer as a result of certain things. But if they just read the popular press view, if they're not involved with the process, they don't understand some of the things that happen as a result.

A large proportion of parents and pupils are Muslims, most originating from Asia, and there was a view that this made a difference to the school in terms of gender issues, particularly in a tendency for girls and boys to work and play apart from each other (hardly unusual in any school). It should be emphasised here, though, that those staff who had the experience of working in other schools were all of the view that the gender problems encountered in Netley Primary were no worse than in any other school, and, to a large extent, were considerably less marked. There was absolutely no sense in which we felt we were responding to a 'special need'. Rather, we were investigating solutions to everyday, commonplace and universal behaviour, and seeking appropriate curricular interventions.

However, in the situation of the predominance of Asian culture within the school we felt that there were a number of traps to be avoided. First of all:

> T: We have to be careful not to stereotype the enormous range of opinions amongst parents.

The second potential trap could be that the (perhaps groundless) fear of causing offence could lead to inaction in matters where girls are clearly being educationally disadvantaged at school:

> T: So it's just an excuse for not tackling it.

The article by Brah and Minhas (1985) was the one article amongst the booklet of readings which nearly all teachers commented on. Everyone who mentioned it found it challenging, and many had sought it out, although it was near the end of the booklet, to read first. Perhaps this is indicative of a concern to understand, to 'get it right', not to be guilty of any of the many pitfalls which beset us in this situation. Gender does not exist alone, and it would be a mistake to interpret gender as an isolated issue and fail to see the perspectives lent by the dimensions of race, culture, religion, language and class. Just recognising that is hard enough. Getting it right, if such a thing is possible, takes longer.

Conclusion

1. The interviews were a useful way of starting: it enabled us subsequently to pay attention to what staff had said they felt unsure about as well as provoking discussion in the areas where they felt more confident.

2. This in turn enabled us to more easily identify where we were up to as a staff and once interest had been gathered we were easily able to involve them in the many other strands of the project as it developed.

3. Giving staff time for reading was really important. They accepted the project as providing necessary professional development and as giving them at least some food for thought.

CHAPTER FIVE

Children as Researchers

Lindsey Lampard

Background

I fell into the Gender Action Project by accident. Although we all knew about it as a staff and I thought it sounded interesting, I had not worked out what particular part I would play in it, if any. When I took over another teacher's class at the half term of the Spring Term I decided that it would be a good idea if I took over the project which had been designed for that class.

Class 6 was going to be an interesting class to observe and discuss gender issues with because of the way the class was behaving. They were the oldest class – twenty-five Year 6 pupils and five Year 5 pupils. They had been taught by a male teacher until November when he was called upon to be the acting headteacher. They then had a succession of supply teachers including a temporary job-share. The acting headteacher had been teaching at Netley Primary for a number of years and was a popular figure with children and parents alike. The children had looked forward to being in his class and were quite upset and resentful when he was called away from them. Added to this, three new boys joined the class and the dynamics of the class changed greatly during this very unsettled time. It was felt that it would be best if I took over teaching them for a number of reasons:

1   I had taught most of them when they were in Year 4, so with the exception of the new children, I knew them and their families very well.

2   I would be with them full-time so there would not be the opportunity to play one teacher off against the other, or for things to be forgotten or not followed through in the changeover. For example, if they misbehaved on Monday morning they would have

to live with the consequences of their actions through until Friday afternoon!

3   It was felt that for the overall good of the school the oldest class must not be in a state of heightened anxiety as the effects of that would permeate down the school.

There were only four weeks before the Easter holidays. This was a very useful settling down period. It was a tough time for all of us because I had to re-establish control: quite simply they had to behave properly or lose certain privileges. I was open with them about how I felt about their behaviour and how other people perceived them as a class, which was not very complimentary. The atmosphere had been very aggressive and many of the children felt threatened. Analysis of the class revealed that six individuals (boys) were at the root of this situation and because of their macho and mocking manner, the rest of the class were either retreating into themselves and not daring to say anything for fear of being laughed at, or they were joining in. The girls fell into two groups – they were either loud and flirtatious to fit in with this group of boys, or they completely retreated and said nothing to anyone. There was another group of boys who also retreated and kept themselves to themselves.

My aim was to settle the whole class down and then begin to challenge and redress the balance of power. I wanted to make space for individuals so that each of them felt secure enough to participate fully in the curriculum. The Gender Action Project could not have come at a better time: whilst as part of the project the children started to observe gender issues in other classes and the school as a whole, I was trying to make life fairer within our class. It was not obvious that the pupils noticed the connections or that they recognised some of their behaviour as sexist. They talked freely about some things being sexist but I did not think they understood the term. They used it to mean not sitting, playing or mixing with the opposite sex. They did not see it as an issue of fairness or power and I thought it would be interesting to see whether as a result of the project they came to understand the term more fully. At one stage I actually said to the class that they all knew what racism was and they would be really shocked if I said it was all right for them to be racist, but that they do not actually take sexism as seriously, and they needed to understand why it is as important and as serious as racism.

Before the class could embark on the project there were some basic issues of class management that I had to address in order for the class to be ready to get fully involved. Firstly I had to set the ground rules, and they had to appreciate how firmly they were set. They knew I would follow up all bad behaviour. They also knew that I would not hesitate to talk to their families if they persisted in aggressive behaviour. My preferred way of dealing with children is in partnership with families and to get to know and talk to families in an informal way on a very regular basis rather than only call them in when there is a problem. That way, when there is a problem, I already have a relationship with the family which makes things easier. One of the first things I did was meet the families of the new children.

The next thing I needed to do was tackle the environment of the class. I reorganised the seating so that the majority of the class felt safe and secure and I isolated those who were dominating and whose behaviour was unacceptable. Initially the children chose their own groups. Ironically the most aggressive and demanding group of children (six boys) chose to sit together. This was good for the rest of the class but before long they were desperate to be split up. They could not cope with competing with each other as they were each used to getting their own way. Through negotiation with the rest of the class these boys were split up and re-seated. Some groups did not change at all, but some agreed to have one of this group of six on their table. It tended to be the strong friendship groups who agreed to additions, as they felt secure enough to deal with the change. There were occasions when an individual child sat alone either through choice or the need to be isolated.

I also introduced a system of credits and privileges. I wanted to be able to praise the children freely and use positive reinforcement to encourage changes in behaviour and attitude. I also wanted a system where the rewards and benefits of good behaviour were as clear as the punishments and disadvantages of bad behaviour.

Friday afternoons were set aside for free choice for those whose behaviour and work deserved such a reward. This time provided some interesting perspectives on gender − the boys, for example, happily chose sewing if it was on offer already, but never requested it. Likewise, the girls used the tools (saws etc) if I put them out but never asked for them if I did not provide them. However girls would find the sewing equipment if it was not out already and the boys would get the tools.

When we came back after Easter, the class had settled down and were less aggressive and mocking. The quieter children were beginning to grow in confidence and were starting to offer answers and make suggestions. They were also beginning to stand up for themselves and I was not having to constantly intervene for them. Before this, I seemed to be continually telling one group of children, not always boys, that they were speaking in an unacceptable way to another group or individual.

As the class were growing in confidence about their individual rights it was a good time to examine gender issues. The plan was to look at different aspects of school life and to decide whether they were fair, and to reflect on different situations to see if they could be improved.

The project

We were very lucky because as part of our involvement, money was made available to us to help with the project. This meant that there were two of us working with the class, myself and a colleague. It was a terrific boon to have a teacher-pupil ratio of one to fifteen, and opportunities to work with small groups to discuss work in depth without the usual demands which normally pull teachers in all directions.

Before we started the project we gave the children a questionnaire to fill in. We wanted to ask them questions which were gender-related, but we did not want to influence their answers. We thought that if we gave them the questionnaire after we had started the project this might affect the way the children answered the questions. There might be an element of 'teacher pleasing' in their answers. We asked them:

> What do you think it is like to be a girl or boy in Class 6? (Good things and bad things).
>
> What do you think it is like to be a woman or a man? (Good things and bad things).

The children answered the question that referred to their own sex first. Then they tried to put themselves in the shoes of a person of the opposite sex. They were allowed to discuss their answers, because we felt that discussion might stimulate ideas rather than the children sticking to 'safe' responses. As is often the case, the omissions were as interesting as the replies, for example some boys did not (or could not) fill in the section 'bad things about being a girl'. Class discussions followed the completion of the questionnaires.

The girls' responses to being a girl in Class 6 were the positive value of sharing things, helping people, talking about 'important things' like religion or people's problems, of not being rude. They saw as negative in being a girl: being bossed about by boys, not being allowed (by the boys) to play football, not having space in the playground, doing more work in the home, not being allowed to go out to play as often as their brothers, of being thought of as weak by boys and being 'sexually abused' (further investigation revealed that the girl meant 'harassed' rather than 'abused'). One girl said a bad thing about being a girl is that girls are 'too kind and helpful'.

The boys described the good things about being a girl as that they got more gifts than boys, particularly jewellery, that they were kind, quiet, polite, never argued, that girls get their own way, don't get told off often, can have long hair and wear make-up. They saw the bad things about being a girl as being pushed around by boys, not being allowed to play football, that all-girls' schools didn't have as many facilities as boys' schools, that girls were fussy, that parents would not allow girls to go to mixed schools 'because they are afraid'.

The boys saw the positive things about being a boy as playing football, being able to choose what secondary school to go to, that when you grow up you are more likely to be successful than a woman, not having to wear a hat for swimming, being good at sport, not needing to look after children all day. The negative things were having lots of fights, being told off, not being able to have your ears pierced, having to sit next to girls, being banned from favourite activities such as football as a punishment, people (especially teachers) believing girls over boys if there is an argument or fight, being teased by other boys, not being allowed to wear make-up.

The girls saw the good things about being a boy as not needing to do the housework and getting more presents or money. They saw the bad things as being made to sit with girls, showing off and having to fight. Interestingly the girls did not put themselves in the boys' shoes but continued to answer the questions as they were affected by them: they wrote that bad things about being a boy are they are noisy, they pick on girls and are sexist. They did not consider bad things that happen to boys, but the bad things that boys do to girls.

Some of the most poignant observations were that 'I hate being a boy because sometimes I *have* to stick up for boys' − the inference being that he did not always want to. Another boy recorded 'I sometimes get nervous when I talk to girls'.

When they came to imagine themselves as adults the girls said the good things about being women would be: looking after children, being able to carry a baby for nine months, helping people, having an easy life and playing with children. The bad things were cooking, washing, cleaning and doing all the housework for the family, having a hard life, working seventeen hours a day, having to carry a baby for nine months. The boys felt the good things about being a woman were 'they get to go out more than men because they have more friends than men', and 'you get lots of respect'. The bad thing about being a woman was being mugged. Very few boys filled in this part of the questionnaire.

Only one boy wrote anything good about being a man and that was if you were a man teacher you got lots of money! Many boys wrote that the bad things about being a man are having to work all day to support your family and having to pay bills. The girls said the good things about being a man were not having to do the housework and having an easy life. They said the bad things about being a man were having to go to work and working a sixteen hour day.

The questionnaire proved a useful opening for discussions about gender issues. As a class teacher I gained a number of insights from some of the answers. It was interesting to see how they viewed life; one boy suggested it was better to be a boy than a girl because you could do more things but when you grew up it was better to be a woman than a man because women had more friends, went out more and had more fun. The other boys at his table agreed with this analysis.

The next stage was for my colleague to come into the class and observe them at work. We decided a science session would be a useful period to observe because I was interested to see how easily the girls were able to participate fully in the practical sessions. Were they able to have their fair share of time with the equipment or were the boys dominating the session? Aside from gender issues, at a management level, were they on task? Was the work holding their interest when I was not actually with that group? A rumour went round the class that they were being observed prior to me writing their reports with the result that they all got on with their work for the whole afternoon and their concentration span was much longer than usual. Although this possibly may have destroyed any 'gender observations', it did provide us with a concrete example of observation to discuss with the class. We examined the purposes of observation, the effects the observer's presence has, the importance of anonymity and how to remain objective. We wanted the children to begin to see what makes a fair test. As they themselves were observed they could draw on first hand experience to discuss these points.

Then we started to move towards the children conducting their own investigations. We ran a pilot as a whole class looking at our school. This gave us the opportunity to question what we were doing, how, why, and the effect we were having on the results. At this stage as teachers we were continually trying to make the children aware of the need for a fair test as required by National Curriculum Attainment Targets in Science.

We then put the children into pre-planned groups: three all boys, two all girls and one mixed group. The mixed group was a group who had chosen to be mixed. In the light of the class background I wanted the children in groups in which they would feel comfortable so that they could produce the best work rather than waste time on in-fighting. We gave the groups a worksheet to help them decide and guide their thinking about what it was about girls and boys they were going to investigate and some of the groups split into sub-groups to make the organisation of the work easier.

Once the children had decided on an area of investigation they began to collect data. Some groups conducted pilot studies to iron out any difficulties in actually collecting information and during the time they were conducting their research, my colleague and I were both on hand to question them, discuss with them and encourage them to explore beyond the obvious. We had sessions with individual groups to discuss how far they had got, so as to decide how best to collate and present their results and to consider how to proceed. We were interested in what they thought should happen as a result of their findings and to constantly examine whether their methods were fair and how, if at all, they could be improved. Alongside this we were doing lots of maths work on sets and pictorial representations, so that they were aware of different forms of expressing results. The project gave the maths work we were doing a very real and relevant purpose. The children also had the opportunity to work on the computer to produce their graphs.

All-girls group 1

The all-girls group decided to investigate how teachers talk to boys and girls. They wanted to find out whether girls or boys got told off or praised more often, whether they were told off or praised for the same things, and how often girls and boys were chosen to answer questions. The girls sat in the back of various classrooms to collect their data. One girl wrote afterwards: 'We thought the teachers might talk nicely with the children, but they acted normally.' They were surprised that the staff continued to tell children off in their presence. In fact, to avoid the 'Hawthorn Effect', when the observers' presence affects the outcome, the staff had agreed to remain in ignorance about the subject of the research until after it was completed. This demonstrates how crucial it was that the whole staff supported the project.

The girls observed in three different classes. They counted the number of times a teacher spoke to a child; whether they were angry or pleased or whether simply asking a question. The children felt that more girls behaved 'in a naughty way' and were told off more. However there were more girls than boys in the classes they observed which had to be taken into account. Also the children doing the observing found it difficult to distinguish between mild and more serious tellings-off. It would be interesting to know whether teacher observations would have yielded the same results. I was trying to discover through discussion with the observation group whether they felt boys and girls were told off for the same things. They found this concept too difficult; as far as they were concerned a telling-off was a telling-off.

The conclusions the girls came to as a result of their observations was that 'girls and boys should be spoken to in the same way and treated the same way.'

At one part in the project the class had a supply teacher while I was at a GAP meeting. When I came back this all-girls' group presented me with tally-chart they had kept during the day to demonstrate how much more the supply teacher had spoken to the boys than to the girls! They had done this totally spontaneously and were outraged at their 'unfair treatment'. As a result of the girls' findings, I believe it would be a useful activity for all class teachers to keep a tally-chart on themselves for a few days just to check their own questioning strategies.

The girls' turned their tally charts into graphs both manually and on the computer. This was a tremendous bonus as it gave their maths work real relevance. They were very personally involved in sorting out how to get their results presented in the best possible way. They certainly covered the National Curriculum Attainment Targets for data-handling and pictorial representation at levels 4 and 5 in maths as a result of this work.

All-boys group 1

This group split into two. Two of the boys observed children playing in the playground; they chalked large squares on the ground in the infants' playground and then observed and recorded what happened in the squares.

They both discovered that the infants mostly stuck to single sex groupings and that the boys ran around more. 'Most of the girls weren't running around a lot like the boys, they were sitting, colouring or talking'. They observed that 'more boys were being bad to the girls than the girls being bad to the boys.' They also said 'it is not fair for the girls because the boys usually were filling up the bench and the girls sat on the floor.'

Both observers enjoyed watching and recording the infants at play.

They both said on several occasions that they found it interesting. I felt that they were very distant and detached from what they observed. They did not relate it to issues of play in the junior playground at all but rather saw it as very separate from their lives. They came up with several practical suggestions as to how to improve the playtimes: have more benches and maybe some tables to do colouring on, have different playgrounds or areas of playground marked out for different things (a quiet playground and areas for football, skipping and chasing games).

The second part of this group chose to observe what reception children talk about. Their predictions proved to be very different from reality. Before they went into the reception class they worked out some categories of conversations and they thought the reception children would talk about 'My little pony', and 'the Turtles' would figure largely. When they went into the reception class they found that none of the children spoke about the things in their categories. They were surprised to discover that most of the time the children were working or talking about work. There are two aspects worth noting here: firstly their own memories of the reception class were inaccurate and secondly, the reception class teacher said that the observers had caused the children to work much harder than usual.

After this initial observation the group re-designed their data collection sheet and went into the reception class for a second time. They discovered that 'girls have better behaviour than boys'. They felt that: 'the reason for this could be their parents' attitude and behaviour.' They recommended that for girls and boys to behave equally well in the future, they should 'work in mixed groups and in partnership together' ·and that 'the teacher should treat people very well but the boys slightly worse to make it equal.' I never did manage to understand this particular piece of logic. They also suggested that 'boys should behave when they are told off so that they will be treated the same.'

It was a good experience for the older children to mix with the reception class, in the younger children's environment, because of what they learnt about the younger children. They enjoyed being with the reception class and began to respect them in a way that perhaps would not have happened if they had only met each other in the playground. One of the boys in the observation group drew a picture to decorate his write-up of a girl and a boy shaking hands and saying 'Lets play yeh' with the caption 'Things should be like this in the future'. I felt that the level of awareness of gender issues had really grown within this group. They, like the all-girls' group were very conscious of what was and was not fair in the treatment of girls and boys.

All-boys group 2

This group also decided to observe how and who children played with in the playground. Part of the group observed in the infants playground and part in the juniors. They made the same recommendations as the other playground group: more benches and special areas for particular activities. They also found that children tended to stick to single-sex groups although there was some mixing.

They recorded certain difficulties they came across during their observations; one was that the infants kept coming up to them and asking what they were doing: 'The funny thing I found out was infants were not easy to handle' one boy wrote. Another boy recorded that at first no-one would go in the chalk boxes they had marked out: 'The squares my friend and I drew may have put people off because they think they're not allowed in them.' All of these difficulties gave the children plenty to discuss and resolve and provided useful material for deciding whether or not they were conducting a fair test and how it could have been improved, all of which forms part of the National Curriculum requirements for science.

All-girls group 2

The second all-girls' group spent a week observing Year 1 children at tidying up time. They wanted to find out if there were any gender differences in who helped tidy up. The girls each observed four children. Every morning of that week the Year 1 teacher gave the children coloured stars to wear, to make it easier for the girls to identify the children they should be observing.

The class teacher was extremely helpful. Every day she arranged to do activities which would create the maximum 'mess'. She also did not intervene during the observation period to discipline pupils who were avoiding the tidying up. This affected the results, of course, but we knew it provided a clearer picture of what happens when the teacher is not looking. The class the girls observed had more boys in it than girls and they found more boys did the tidying up, although many boys 'just wandered around.' One girl wrote 'what I found very funny was that some boys and girls hid when it was tidy-up time.' I think they found it funny that such 'little children' could be so sneaky to avoid tidying-up. However they were very struck by the unfairness of the situation. They had different suggestions as to how to make the tidying-up fairer. One said 'in the future there should be a girl and a boy tidying up together'. Another wrote 'In the future the teacher should have a rota.'

Before they began their observations the girls felt that the girls would do most of the tidying up. It was not clear whether this was a reflection of our own class or life in general. When they did their observations it seemed as if they had been proved wrong; that the boys were doing the most. We then had to do some more work on averages and percentages (more National Curriculum Attainment Targets) because of the high number of boys to girls in the class we were observing. The group then realised that their predictions had been verified.

One girl decorated her write up with figures of girls and boys alternately in the margin with speech bubbles coming out of their mouths:

Girl: I love tidying up
Boy: I'm tired
Girl: I enjoy it
Boy: Why do I have to do the work?
Boy: I'm not doing anything (drawn with feet on desk sitting on chair)
Girl: I like tidying up
Boy: I hate tidying up
Girl: I like to help
Boy: Too bad, I don't
Girl: I'm tidying up

Does this sum up every classroom at tidying up time?

All-boys group 3

This group divided into two and completed two very different research projects. Two of the boys chose to go to the Toy Library which meets one morning a week in our school hall. They wanted to find out what pre-school children play with and whether girls and boys play with the same toys or if there is already a marked difference.

They discovered that the girls and boys *wanted* to play with the same toys but that it does not always work out that way. One little boy played with a toy train for the whole time despite the fact that some of the girls wanted to play with it. The following is a tape transcript of an interview between a teacher and the pupils conducting the research after observing in the toy library.

P: Miss, he must have liked the train. That's why he wanted to play with it.
T: The boy liked the train, yes, but what about the girls? Do you think the girls wanted to play with the train, too?

84

P: Yes.
T: Why couldn't they?
P: Because a boy was playing with it.
T: Right. Did you see girls actually trying to play with it?
P: Yes.
T: And the boys wouldn't let them.
P: No, Miss and they just ... and they just played.
T: Do you think that was fair?
P: No, Miss.
T: What do you think would have been fairer?
P: If the boys and the girls played with them.
T: What could the people in charge of the Toy Library or the mums there, what could they have done?
P: Get two separate...
P: Give half to the boys and half to the girls.
T: What do you mean, half of what?
P: Get half of ...(indistinct)
T: I see. So you could actually halve the equipment and let boys have some and girls have the other. That's a good idea. Is there anything else that they could do?
P: Miss, they could share it.
T: How could they share?
P: They could play with the same thing.
T: At the same time.
P: Yes.
T: The boy obviously wouldn't do that, would he? He wouldn't let them. Why do you think that is?
P: The boys have more things than the girls. They play the most.
T: Do you think the boy was too young to understand about sharing?
P: Yes.
T: ... and maybe that was the problem ...
P: Miss, he's only two or three years old isn't he? He needs someone to explain to him.

The boys went on in the rest of the interview to make some good suggestions about how to overcome the problems of not wanting to share toys, to sidetrack the child with the offer of a different toy or to have single sex sessions.

P: Miss, he played with other toys but he kept on coming back.
P: Miss, the lady could have said why don't you play with something else or something ... or the bike.

P: Make up four classes. On Monday ten boys could come, on Tuesday ten girls could come. And on Wednesday and Thursday and there would be different classes. So there would be enough toys for them to play with.

T: Oh, right. Have two Toy Libraries, one for boys and one for girls.

Later in the interview the boys acknowledged other problems having single-sex sessions might incur:

P: If the boy's playing with that toy probably the girl wants that toy, well some of the girls might be jealous of what the boys have got and some of the boys might be jealous of what the girls have got.

P: So they've got to keep away from each other.

T: So they've separated it might start making them be more. . .

P: They might get a habit of staying away and be sexist.

T: He's making a good point, he's saying that starts the boys and girls in a bad habit of staying apart and staying separate. Is that what you mean? Yes? I think that's a good point because I think one of the things we might be trying to do, especially when you're looking at children that young is to. . .?

P: Teach them.

T: Yes. And maybe teach that little boy to maybe share a bit. It's not going to happen straight away, but maybe try and encourage him. Do you think that anything like that happens in your class?

P: No.

The boys would not acknowledge that they might be sexist. Each time during the interview that my colleague tried to get them to identify with the behaviour they had observed they changed the subject. When they tried to give examples of how hard they worked and how they weren't sexist like the pre-school children they observed it back-fired on them:

P: Because Miss we've been taught not to thingy . . . be bad, been taught not to be racist or sexist, whatever and so that's why, miss coz we've been taught to be. . .

T: So you don't think that some of the things that the girls say are true, then, I mean the girls say, some of the girls say, that the boys don't tidy up as much as the girls. Do you think that. . .

P: Miss, that can't be true because, just say at home the boys tidy up more than the girls at home.

T: How do you know?

P: Well it might be. Miss, in some houses everyone has to do the work, like in my house, my dad has to do some work, whatever it is he has to do, like everyone, et cetera, my two little sisters. All the people do the housework.

P: Usually at home people say that more girls do work, but outside home and schools boys do most of the work. And inside home and at my cousins' house girls do most of the work.

T: How do you mean, outside home boys do most of the work?

P: Miss, our relations, whenever someone comes over round our house all the men start speaking and the children go up to the room and start playing.

T: So when people come to your house, who helps your mum, then?

P: Miss, the ladies.

T: And the men sit around talking.

P: Yes.

T: And so who's doing all the work then?

P: Miss, the ladies.

P: Miss, in my house, yeah, right, my brothers and my sisters... but my two sisters have to get up as soon as we've finished dinner they collect all the plates and then they have to take it to the kitchen and wash it up. My mum after that she has to wash it and that and then my sisters have to dry and my brothers just sit there smoking and drinking a cup of coffee.

T: And what about you?

P: I'm in my bedroom playing, Miss.

T: So it's your sisters who do the work and your mum. And do you think it's possible that it makes you less inclined to do stuff when you're at school? Tidying up, washing up paintbrushes, things like that, do you think so?

P: When my mum's friends are over and she wants to talk and or if she doesn't feel like getting up because she's not feeling well she asks me to do all the work around the house I do the hoovering and sometimes I make tea and instead of cooking I just get the microwave.

T: So you do some of the work if there's a reason.

P: Miss in the mornings I have to make breakfast, that is bacon, eggs, tomatoes and scrambled eggs, toast, Miss.

T: That's some breakfast. Every morning?

P: Every single morning, Miss.

Although the group was beginning to observe sexist behaviour they found it difficult to relate it back to themselves.

The second half of this all-boys group decided to find out whether girls have tidier hand-writing than boys. This idea was put forward by one of the boys who himself has enormous difficulties with hand-writing and spelling. My colleague and I found this very interesting as he seemed to be trying to investigate the extent to which his own difficulties were caused by being a boy.

It was difficult to decide what constituted tidy hand-writing and the boys decided somewhat unconvincingly to use the criterion of whether it was joined-up or not. Whilst they were getting the pupils to do a piece of writing they decided to give them a spelling test so that they would be able to see if there were any gender differences in the pupils' ability to spell.

Both of these areas were interesting to investigate. Unfortunately the boys muddled their data to such an extent it was impossible to come to any firm conclusions. They also had immense difficulty in marking the spelling tests because of their own spelling difficulties! As with so many things, we might have been able to sort that data out or re-run the tests, but we were beaten by the clock. This would be an interesting project to do again, to see what conclusions the pupils might come to in relation to gender differences in spelling and hand-writing.

Mixed Group

This group chose to investigate whether age played any part in whether children play with friends of the opposite sex or not. They also wanted to investigate career choices at different ages. It was agreed that they would be able to visit a large local nursery to conduct some of their work. They were very excited by the prospect of this special visit, and one commented: 'They'll think we're those inspectors. . .' (The school had recently had a visit from a member of Her Majesty's Inspectorate and she was referring to that).

The group had to be briefed on talking to very young children, and on the importance of introducing themselves and putting their 'interviewees' at ease. In the event, they were so nervous that only one (a boy) remembered to do so.

All in all they interviewed a small group of children from each of three age groups, nursery, Year 1 and Year 5. They asked all the children who their friends were, and later observed the same children at play to see if the results of the interviews were confirmed by reality. They also asked the children what they would like to be when they grew up.

The information on careers did not show any particular pattern, although the group were amused that a girl in the nursery wanted to be a 'postman', which provided a valuable teaching point. Since the girls for the most part wanted to be lawyers, doctors and teachers, we felt they were not underselling themselves!

The results showed that nursery children played more in mixed groups and named more friends of the opposite sex. One boy wrote afterwards: 'The funny thing about the nursery children was that they said their best friends were their own sex, but they played in mixed groups.' Pupils in Year 1 played more in single sex groups and named no friends of the opposite sex. Pupils in Year 5 came in between.

The group had not expected these results. They had thought the oldest children would have been the most sexist:

G: Miss, we thought Class 5 would be more sexist because they're older and they know what it means and everything.

T: When you say they 'know', what do you mean?

G: They know what it means.

T: They know that there's some of ...

G: Miss they know all the, oh boys can play better and all this ... so we might as well play together because we always used to see them playing football, boys or men, but then after that they used to get ladies on and it was a ladies match.

T: So. Are you saying that girls don't play with boys because they're not as good as boys?

G: No. Boys. I thought they might be the most sexist because all the games that they play always seem to be involving men.

B: Miss now, everyone plays marbles.

T: And that's since football was banned.

G: Nothing else to do.

G: Miss, some people play cricket.

G: Sometimes we just join in a cricket game and no-one notices.

T: And is that all-girls or mixed?

G: Mixed but mostly girls.

T: When you say nobody notices, who could notice that you'd joined in the cricket?

G: Miss we just run round and just look at the game and someone will get the ball and throw it to us and if we catch the ball lots of times they say OK you can play.

T: So you have to show that you can catch the ball first. Certainly you found that there's not much playing in mixed groups. Do you think anything should be done about that? Is there something we should do as teachers?

They were very unsure about how teachers could help them mix better in the playground. They were all in agreement that mixing more should be encouraged:

T: What are the good things about mixing?
G: Have more fun?
T: Get used to each other.
G: To get on. To know each other.

After the investigations

Once all the groups had collected their data, discussed their findings and written up their accounts we decided to make a video of their work. We wanted a record of what they had chosen to investigate, what they had found out and the recommendations for change they were proposing. Making a video gave the project an added interest to the class. They were very excited about seeing themselves on the screen and in many ways it gave the work a higher status in their eyes (See Chapter Six).

The majority of the class left for their different secondary schools at the end of term. Some went to single-sex schools, the majority went to the mixed school close to our catchment area. My colleague and I invited the children back the following Autumn Term to watch the finished version of the video. They had seen parts of it at different stages but we felt it would make a neat conclusion to GAP if we had an evening when we invited the children and their parents to come back and view the video and see all their work displayed.

We provided refreshments and it was a good opportunity for them to meet up again as they had now split into at least five different schools. After they had watched the video we asked them to complete a questionnaire. We wanted to try to find out whether the project had made any long term changes to the children's perceptions.

We did not discuss the questions with them but let them fill them in either privately or in their new school groups (they could choose) because we did not want to influence them in any way. The questions and a selection of answers can be found in Appendix D.

Conclusions

The project could not have come at a better time. The class learnt enormously from it. They now understood that the term sexist meant more than simply not sitting or playing in mixed groups. Overall, I could see from class discussions and informal conversation that many of the class particularly the girls, had learnt that sexism is to do with power and fairness.

Through the GAP the children learnt that aspects of school life are not fair in terms of gender. They had the chance to reflect on those facts and make suggestions as to how things could be improved. Many of the children became very fired up about issues of fairness. They had progressed in the sense that they now recognised inequalities and had some language to describe what they felt was happening. They offered some useful solutions to many of the issues raised. They also improved as individuals and as a class during the time of the project. I felt very positive about GAP because the children responded so well to it. They did not see the difficulties as insurmountable. The class was looking at gender issues with fresh eyes and were optimistic that most of the problems could be solved. Those of us with more experience however might be forgiven for believing that it might not be so easy.

I think GAP was special: all of us who were involved found it interesting and inspiring. This is probably why it snowballed in the way it did and grew into something much bigger than we had originally thought it would be. It was cross-curricular and covered many of the National Curriculum Programmes of Study for English, Maths, Science and Information Technology.

One of the key factors that came out of doing the GAP was how easy it was to meet the National Curriculum Attainment Targets through the work. We covered all the English Attainment Targets at Level Four and in addition many Maths and Science Attainment Targets.

In the future it will be vital for me to ensure that gender issues are central in my own planning. In general, through my involvement in GAP it has become clear to me that in these highly pressured days of the National Curriculum, unless gender education is integral to all aspects of the curriculum, with the best will in the world it will be sidelined and ultimately lost. 'Gender' cannot be seen as something you tag on to other areas but should underpin the whole curriculum. Gender issues should not just be about classroom organisation they should be part of the curriculum too.

Finally

I would like to thank the rest of the staff and children at school without whom we would not have had a GAP. They put up with being observed, questioned, made to wear large badges, and the general comings and goings while the research was being completed.

CHAPTER SIX

A Lesson Using The National Curriculum

Marjorie Smith

In July 1991, most of Class 6 left Netley Primary School to go on to secondary school. In some ways, my colleague and I regretted having undertaken the project with the oldest pupils in the school, because we could not watch their 'gender awareness' developing, or fully judge the outcome of our work. Perhaps this was a mistake. In retrospect, though, I have come to the conclusion that one big project is relatively ineffectual unless it forms part of a whole school, on-going programme of gender work. Looking at it from that point of view, we had only just begun.

In September 1991, my colleague went back to the Infant Department to teach a Year two (top infant) class. I was by then working in a job-share, teaching a mixed class of Year 4 and Year 5 pupils. We were thus in an ideal position to work across a wider age range, and perhaps to engage the interest of more teachers in the school.

We were determined to show that gender work can be done within all the National Curriculum subject areas. It became increasingly clear throughout our time of working with Class 6 (and also through the regular meetings we had at the Teachers' Centre, with the GAP group) that the National Curriculum is a valuable focusing point for gender. This is not because the National Curriculum gives some sort of spurious validity to gender work. I strongly contend that gender stands on its own as an essential component of any educational philosophy. Rather, the interlinking of gender with the National Curriculum helped us to see that it could all be done, despite the pressures. In our earlier project, we had focused on the National Curriculum in Mathematics. This year we wanted to explore a wider range of subject areas. During the course of the year we focused on gender in History with Drama, Science, and Design and Technology with English. This chapter tells what we did.

Another teacher who had previously attended a drama course

concentrating on gender issues, also became involved in the project. We had asked her to take a drama session with Class 6 which we attempted to video. We were electrified. Here was a skilled practitioner in drama using her skills to make points within a few minutes which we were still struggling to put across. Drama – hitherto a somewhat mediocre part of my repertoire – was a powerful tool in this teacher's hands. Thus she joined the project and agreed to do some work with her own class. It became apparent that we did not have the skills to video a useful session ourselves and as we felt it was essential to use this medium, we involved the borough's Media Resources Unit. There can be so much happening in drama which is difficult to portray on paper and we thought that a good video could be a valuable tool in the professional development of teachers. In the process of this work the pupils had the opportunity to make their own videos.

The drama teacher undertook to cover gender through History in the National Curriculum. Her class had just completed a term's work on 'Victorian Britain' and were about to embark on the Core Study Unit of 'Explorers and Encounters 1450 to 1550'. In just the one session, she explored the children's attitudes to Victorian women, to 'explorers' in general, and then to one woman Victorian explorer, Mary Kingsley. The drama teacher's work is not described in this book, but the video which she made with the professional support of others in Waltham Forest, showing a number of drama techniques being used in the exploration of gender issues, is now being used for staff development. (Freeman 1992).

My colleague's work with a top infant class concerned looking at differences between familiar things. In the National Curriculum document for Science in use at the time, this work formed part of Science, Level Two, Attainment Target 2a): 'Be able to sort familiar living things into broad groups according to easily observable features'. The topic was 'Ourselves', and covered some aspects of similarities and differences between boys and girls, and men and women. She made use of a pack called 'When I Grow Up...' which had been produced by the Careers Service of the LEA. This pack consists of several large, plastic-backed colour photographs of local people in non-stereotypical roles: an Asian policewoman, a black woman bus driver, a black woman doctor, a male nurse, a black male nursery nurse, a black male headteacher and a male homemaker, among others. The pack includes job descriptions and teacher's notes.

My colleague developed the idea of careers by asking the children what they wanted to be when they grew up. She only introduced the photographs after some discussion. There were some interesting gender differences in the children's responses to the photographs. Boys who had made career choices which were depicted in the photographs were slightly disturbed to see women in the careers they had chosen for themselves. One boy said that he wanted to be a 'busman' (further questioning elicited the information that he specifically wanted to be a bus driver). Looking at the photograph of a woman bus driver, he was most insistent that he had never seen a 'busmanlady' and that he wanted to be a 'busman', not a 'busmanlady'. Some boys also refused to accept the pictures for what they were. The male childminder in the photograph, for example, was definitely a dad bringing his child to the house (the explanation was that the woman childminder was still inside the house!).

Girls did not seem to be affected by the sight of a man in a role they had chosen for themselves. For some reason, the picture of the nurse was in another classroom. The girl who wanted to be a nurse sought out the picture of the male nursery nurse, as being the closest thing to what she wanted, and was totally unaffected to find that the picture portrayed a man. Some girls actually changed their career choices to a traditionally male dominated career after seeing the photographs. One girl decided that she wanted to be a telecommunications engineer rather than a hairdresser, and another that she wanted to be a 'milkie', when her previous career choice had been to be a mother. None of the boys changed their choices.

The sexist language used to describe adult employment was discussed (for example 'postman'/'postperson', 'milkman'/'milkperson'). The girls were much more open to the idea of changing traditional terms than the boys, who seemed to resist any change. Overall, the discussion of language was an uphill climb, perhaps more appropriate to an older age group.

The pack proved to be a very useful resource, and one which could be used in a number of valuable ways for gender work. I went on to use the photographs of the woman architect and the woman builder for my class topic on 'Buildings' with my class of Year four and Year five pupils. The class contrasted the photographs with the definitions of these careers to be found in our rather dated school dictionaries. An architect, for example, was defined as '. . . a man who designs buildings . . .'

With the same class and as part of the same topic, I set out to design a project in Design and Technology which would address some gender issues. I bore in mind the issues raised in previous chapters and the need to make 'male' subjects, such as Design and Technology, more 'girl-friendly'. I focused on 'The Playground' as an aspect of the built environment, and small groups of pupils were asked to design playgrounds for each other. The pupils were put in single-sex groups of three or four, based largely on friendship groupings, but ensuring a reasonable spread of ability, so that every group included at least one pupil who could read and write with ease. Each group of girls was then paired off with a group of boys. I determined these 'pairings', and ensured that there was a racial mix in the final pairs of groups. Each girls' group was asked to design a playground for the boys based on the boys' expressed requirements, and each boys' group was asked to design a playground for the girls, based on their preferences. The implications of these groupings are discussed later.

At the time of planning this project, I was under the impression that I would be covering only the Attainment Targets in the Design and Technology National Curriculum. After the project was over, however, when I was going through the National Curriculum to complete our records, I realised just how many English Attainment Targets had been covered very thoroughly during the project, because of the amount of consultation that was required within groups and across groups. In summary, the project covered the following Attainment Targets in force at the time: Design and Technology, Level Three, Attainment Targets 1a), b), 2a), 3a), b), d), 4a), b); Level Four, Attainment Targets 1c), 2), 3b), 4a), English, Level Three, Attainment Targets 1b), c), d); Level Four; Attainment Targets 1b), c).

The pupils were required to:

- discuss and agree their playground requirements with other members of their group

All the group members worked together, with one scribe, to produce some ideas to which they all agreed.

- interview their client group initially, and consult with members of the group throughout the duration of the project as matters arose

Group members had to plan a series of questions, interview their 'clients', and record the answers.

- visit a local playground, make observational drawings of the equipment, make a plan of the layout, discuss other aspects of playground design, such as safety, and access for children with disabilities

All the children, working in pairs, used a local map to find a direct route. On the way they were asked to consider the difficulties a wheelchair user might encounter using the same route. The playground we visited had a safety surface and ramps which provided points for discussion. We looked at how the playground equipment was set in the ground, and considered what the swings, see-saws and climbing frames were made of. One of the items of equipment was a climbing frame shaped like an artillery tank, which provided a useful discussion point about weapons of war as playthings, and gave the opportunity to discuss whether this playground was designed with boys or girls in mind.

- make observations of children of the opposite sex in the playground to determine their preferred activities, draw a graph to show results and make inferences from collated information from the whole class

In one playtime the entire class observed the rest of the school at play. The children had drawn up a list of playground activities beforehand. They simply put a tick against the activities that each girl or boy was seen doing. The activities were: playing with a ball, talking, playing marbles, running, skipping with a rope, standing (not talking) and hopscotch. Afterwards they drew up their own bar charts to show what they had seen. I then produced another graph from all their observations, from which it was possible to make comparisons between girls and boys. In fact, there was very little difference between the sexes for all of the activities except skipping with a rope. Although more boys than girls were seen running, and more girls than boys were observed to be talking, the fact was that these two activities were engaged in most by both sexes.

- draw up a plan of the group's design, based on their client group's wishes

The plan was to be the same size as the eventual model.

- reassess the plan on the basis of financial, safety and access considerations, with consultation with the client group

I gave each group a list of approximate costs for buildings (e.g. toilets), items of playground equipment, swimming pools and changing rooms (very popular on the original plans), seats, ramps for prams and wheelchair users, safety surface, non-safety surface and grass. Each group was then given a ceiling price and told they had to work within that budget. The budget was different for each group because I did not want them to have to make too many fundamental changes to their original designs. The intention on this occasion was to encourage a discussion about needs and priorities, not to limit the children's ideas. Most groups made cuts in costs by combining separate buildings (e.g. toilets for girls and boys) into one unit, or reducing the numbers of seats or items of playground equipment. All the groups retained ramps and safety surfaces, despite the additional costs.

- make a scale model of the final plan, with at least one moving part, selecting appropriate materials, adhesives, etc, from a range of those available

Each group used a piece of stiff card for a base. The following were freely available: wood, paper, card, plastic sheeting, paint, Copydex, Blu-Tack, Pritt Stick, PVA adhesive, split pins, paperclips, pipecleaners. I identified the materials which were expensive, and made clear at the outset that overuse or unfair use of those materials would lead to an adverse evaluation. The nature of the model was such that it was possible to delegate tasks to individual members of each group, and it was made clear that everyone should have definite 'job', but each person was responsible for consulting the others in the group, as well as the client group.

- each group to evaluate the model made by that group, and each group to evaluate the model designed for that group.

Before the models were finished, I gathered the whole class together and evaluated each model both as a playground and as a model. I commented on aesthetic appeal, scale and design. The most common mistakes were those of scale. I also assessed choice of materials in making the model, and whether it was well put together or not. Overuse of Blu-Tack predominated, and one or two children had used inappropriate adhesives (for example, Pritt Stick to hold pieces of wood together). There was also a tendency to use bits of junk which looked good on the model, but would have been quite out of place in a life-size playground. Some aspects of the model-making were really excellent. The children made working swings and roundabouts and slides, and quite a few models sported swimming pools with diving boards.

I felt this teacher-led session was very important in letting the pupils know what I was expecting of them when it came to the evaluation stage. After this, they had time to make amendments to their models and much Blu-Tack was returned.

After this, every pupil had to evaluate two things − his or her own model, and secondly, the playground designed for his or her group. All the pupils were encouraged to say *why* they liked or disliked something, and to suggest an alternative if possible.

These are some examples from their evaluations.

Of the models the pupils made:

'I like the slide because it looks like a real slide. I don't like the swings because they are wobbly.' (girl)

'I don't like the safety surface because it is too dark.' (girl)
'I don't like the bin because it is too big.' (boy)

Of the playground designs made to pupils specifications:

'The boys (the clients) don't like the pond because it is dangerous for babies.' (girl)
'I would build a fence around the pond with a gate for big people.' (boy)
'I like the tree because I can climb it.' (boy)
'I would put a football pitch instead of the Punch and Judy show.' (boy)
'I would put the swimming pool in the corner.' (girl)
'The toilets are taking up too much space.' (boy)

The children were also asked to consider their designs in relation to our existing playground which at that time was very small, but was extended in the summer of 1992:

'We have only got dustbins ... I would like grass and trees in my playground.' (boy)
'It would be better because in our playground there is nothing but plain gravel (asphalt).' (boy)
'We would like our playground to be bigger, and we would like everything we chose that the boys made.' (girl)

I allocated one afternoon a week to this project, although some of the discussion work and mathematics work took place in the mornings. On this basis the entire project took only half a term. I can say without reservation that all the pupils, girls and boys, benefitted in terms of their skills in Design and Technology.

In relation to gender, it is worth relating an incident which happened with this class at the beginning of the year, before the project began. During a drama session, as part of the topic on 'Buildings', we talked about the reasons why people might want to move house and the reasons why they might not want to move. I wanted the pupils to pretend to be a man and a woman discussing the reasons why they should stay in their house, or move. I asked everyone to pair up with a member of the opposite sex, and then to sit down with their partners. The entire class remained standing except for one boy and one girl (the boy had grabbed her and sat down). This went on for ten minutes until I intervened and sorted out the pairs myself. They were then given time to discuss and practise the task. Most of them stared at the ceiling or the walls and did not speak at all: nevertheless all of them wanted to act out their 'scene', which on this occasion, I allowed, despite the lack of preparation. Of the fourteen couples discussing the relative merits and demerits of this home, ten ended up shouting and four ended up pretending to hit one another. When I pointed out to the class that in all four cases it was the 'man' who 'hit' first, I think they were genuinely shocked.

I learnt a great deal from this experience. The fact that the children would not pair up with opposite-sex partners, or talk to each other, was not particularly surprising. It certainly reflected the usual pattern throughout the school, as was made clear from comments teachers made during the interviews described in Chapter 4. Many teachers would recognise this phenomenon, and many would avoid asking pupils to work in mixed-sex pairs for this reason. However, this one incident alerted me to the likely state of classroom interaction between boys and girls, and further observation confirmed that, indeed, boys and girls simply did not talk to each other. The escalation of a discussion into a shouting match probably had many origins, including showing off. However, as I watched, I was convinced that several pupils were having enormous difficulties in expressing themselves orally, and that this was a major area for further work.

When the project began, the announcement that they would be working in single-sex groupings was greeted with resounding cheers from the boys and a polite silence from the girls. Later on into the project, one boy complained that they were having to do 'everything' for girls, and observe girls in the playground, and could they do something for boys next time? Interestingly, he was 'hushed' by both boys and girls. I cannot fully explain this reaction. I had pointed out to the class the reasons for doing the project, and I had told them that I realised that boys and girls hardly spoke to one another, and that I believed that this was something they should be working on. Perhaps some of the class recognised this and agreed with me or perhaps they realised that he had implicitly challenged one of the reasons for doing the project?

Throughout the project, I stressed the importance of consultation. I actually used the terms 'consult' and 'client', and by the end of the project, the pupils were using those terms quite freely, too. I spent a great deal of time checking that each new development in a design had been agreed upon by the entire group and by the clients. Anyone who had failed to do this was sent to do so immediately. Two groups of girls complained that their client groups were being unhelpful, and refusing to answer questions. When this happened, I always suggested they try again and observed the consequences. In both cases the boys tried to brush the girls off, but then realised that I was there and began to respond.

One of the most helpful events in promoting the contact between groups was a visit from an architect. Through connections I have with a group called WARM (Women As Role Models), a group which aims to encourage more girls to enter the construction industry, I was able to contact an architect, who came to talk to the class about her work and to show them some examples of architect-designed buildings. The class were very excited and prepared some questions for the visitor. I was expecting them to be surprised that our visitor was a woman, and indeed they were. One or two boys were good-naturedly amused that 'Miss' had 'done it again', and although we laughed about it together, I think their reaction actually masked genuine shock. When the architect talked about her work, I detected no resistance at all to the idea of a woman designing a building. The class were most interested in the personal side of things. They were very impressed by how much money she earned (as I was), and by the fact that she sometimes has to stay up until three in the morning. I was also pleased that she mentioned having a small child so that the children had access to working mothers as role models, as well as working women in general.

The architect made a major difference to the project. I had not predicted this at all, but after her visit, when she talked about her 'clients' and their demands, the children seemed to 'click' to the notion of designing for someone else, rather than themselves. I was now being very firmly put in my place when I asked about some change to a plan or a model, and why the change had been made. 'Our clients wanted it that way', was the cool reply. The boys, in particular, became very demanding of their clients, insisting on decisions from them. They also ceased to be unhelpful as clients. They realised they were 'paying'.

By the end of the project, the interactions between members of the class took on a totally different pattern. Boy and girls were crossing the room purposefully to make enquiries of each other, or to discuss some aspect of a model. Naturally the work did not end there. I continued to make the best of this improvement through the way I grouped the class for different activities, and in the use of drama. By the end of the year, the requirement to work with a pupil of the opposite sex was commonplace and natural, and the work was completed. Some of the children were even sitting in mixed groups out of choice.

Does it matter if children do not talk to each other? In my view it does if the factor which limits contact is poor communication skills. The pupils here were involved in a legitimate Design and Technology exercise, which demanded a high level of effective verbal communication. As such, this sort of work is vital to their effective learning.

I also think it matters that children do not talk to each other if the limits to effective, purposeful communication are differences in gender, race or ability. The roots of this prejudice may lie in ignorance of each other's needs, aspirations and abilities, and are nurtured by silence and assumption. By promoting purposeful talk across gender, race and ability barriers, we were hoping to promote a better understanding.

In March 1992, the three of us who had been more heavily involved in the project organised a professional development session in school. We talked about all the things we had done in relation to the gender project, the interviews, the project with Class 6, and the follow-up work in History with Drama, Science and Design and Technology with English. The video was shown and we had the 'When I Grow Up' pack and the work from the Class 6 project on display. One development from this has been the emergence of a pilot planning sheet for use by all teachers in all National Curriculum subject areas, in which teachers must identify the ways in which they are dealing with gender, race and disability issues within their National Curriculum subject planning. In this way, I would hope to promote more of the 'curriculum' type of gender work described earlier.

Conclusion

In the Summer Term of that year, we heard that the LEA had been awarded a Positive Action Award from the Fawcett Society, and that this was partly due to our work in the Gender Action Project. I spoke to all the children who had been involved in the various projects in the school, partly to thank them, but also to make the point that *somebody else* thinks that this work is important. The children were thrilled, and I do not doubt for one moment that this sort of external recognition has raised the importance of gender work in the eyes of our girls and our boys, and, hopefully, their carers, parents and families.

Where do we go from here? The list of things we still have to do is now longer than it ever was. As we in the school have become more aware, we have become more sophisticated in the demands we make of ourselves. Presumably this is a never-ending process, and I do not believe that any of us could ever reach that point when we can claim we have 'got it right' because that would be the point when we would cease to struggle. So I, at least , look on that ever-growing list as evidence of our own growth as a group of committed teachers.

A priority on our list of work for the future is to familiarise parents and governors with our work on gender, and to consult them fully on their views regarding priorities and practice. I would hope to take up my colleague's suggestion of a 'curriculum' evening on gender to which parents and governors might be invited, with their children, to look at our resources and perhaps to take part in some activities. This is not the only priority. We have yet, for example, to address the issue of midday assistants and the children's reaction to them.

We have recognised the need to reconsider the topic framework in the light of gender needs, giving more space to topics which demonstrate gender issues more effectively. Similar work is described in the Equal Opportunities Policy (Gender) of Hornimans Primary School, reprinted in Weiner (1990), and the work of the Anti-Sexist Working Party (1985). At Netley Primary, we are currently revising the topic programme in the light of National Curriculum Attainment Targets *and* the demands of our developing programme of Personal, Social and Health Education, which would include gender issues among many others. The final framework will specify when particular Attainment Targets will be covered in most National Curriculum subjects as well as providing a curriculum for PSHE, including gender. This is an opportunity to provide a gender curriculum which can build on children's existing knowledge and ensure that gender permeates all subject areas, as appropriate. It is also an opportunity to ensure that the necessary resources are provided where and when they are required. There will also be a structure to facilitate some input in relation to how activities in Science or Design and Technology are approached, so as to ensure access and relevance for girls.

In this way, by including gender within the topic-based curriculum, and supporting gender work with improved resourcing and guidance *linked to the curriculum,* and to the promotion of appropriate teaching methods, I would hope that marginalisation of gender issues would be avoided. There will be a shift in emphasis for gender, away from focusing on how pupils behave in the school, towards what they should be learning in class as part of the overt curriculum. As a school, we will effectively be developing a curriculum for gender, which will be topic-based, and within which we will be able to introduce new areas of gender work at appropriate stages. We will at last be able to build-in progression, using the opportunities for discussion and reflection which will be created by this. Insecurity as to what is 'right' in gender, which was identified during the interviews and which seems to affect most teachers, could be gradually overcome. By integrating gender into the curriculum, effective contribution to staff development can be made.

At the time of writing, there is still no gender policy for the school, and it seems a long time ago that production of a policy was our sole aim. We are all still in the process of becoming a group of people who are able to contribute to the production of a policy. Our current working policy is here, within these pages, with all its yawning gaps and glaring inadequacies. Having said that, I think we are further forward in our approach to gender than many schools who do have written policies. As a teacher I am committed to the development of whole-school policies, but that genuine commitment is the very thing which makes me hang back. Sometimes the policy is seen as the starting point. Maybe, in some situations, that would be the best way forward. At other times, however, writing a policy is the lesser of many evils when it comes to initiating change, and a way of avoiding the more difficult and more pressing tasks. In this case, I hope to redress the balance, and make up for the occasional policy which I have written which has had minimal impact when it comes to institutional change. The gender policy for this school is alive and well, but as yet unwritten.

CHAPTER SEVEN

What We Have Learned
Ruth Frith and Pat Mahony

When we began the Gender Action Project, our main concern was to develop practices in schools which would significantly alter the quality of the girls' education. We also wanted to work with teachers in ways which were non-authoritarian and which would engage them as professionals in their own development.

It is true that we have learned a great deal about many aspects of trying to change gender relations in schools. Just as important though were the unexpected outcomes. We had not expected, for example, to find a way of working with teachers which was at times inspirational and always exciting. This created its own energy and enthusiasm which not only maintained the project group but in some cases spilled over into the whole school initiative. Perhaps the most important lesson of all is that even while teachers were drowning in yet another wave of Government documentation explaining the latest revision of curriculum content or assessment arrangements, what really engaged them was the model of professional development which underpinned the project.

In this respect who 'owns' the initiative would seem to be crucial and where teachers do, the results can be startling.

It is not the case that extra work involved in the project operated as a 'last straw' − on the contrary. Teachers were in a position of proposing their own tentative solutions to problems which in every case were compatible with the concerns of central Government and what any responsible headteacher with or without the market ideology would espouse, viz. improving the quality of education. But it was the teachers themselves who were in control of framing the problems in ways which made sense in terms of their own practice. This had the effect of releasing energy, commitment and enthusiasm. It is our view that this would not have been the case had we tried to enforce yet another set of prescriptions onto teachers already dispirited and overwhelmed by what they were dealing with.

We learned too of the importance of fully briefing those who were managing the change. It seemed to us that the connection between quality and equality is self evident. The whole point about the movement towards equality, is that no one is proposing that we move to equality of awfulness. Rather *equality of quality* is what is at issue: whether that be increased self-esteem of all pupils, confidence to acquire new skills or the raising of examination results. The problem was that headteachers did not see this as obvious. They felt they had enough to do to achieve quality without doing more work on 'equality'. As one put it, 'I'm more interested in getting children to read than I am in equal opportunities'. We learned very fast to explain the project from their perspective, starting with their preoccupations of raising standards. Once they saw the connection they did become committed. But it did not stop here. It was not enough for us, the project managers, to enlist headteachers' support for the project. Equally important were discussions with the project group about the arguments *they* could use in their schools with senior colleagues and with the benefit of hindsight it would have helped in one case if we had done more of this earlier.

The three way partnership between Higher Education, Local Authority and schools turned out to have real benefits in terms of the relationship between theory and practice. Student teachers can gain a great deal (albeit second hand) from learning about the potential for experienced practitioners to theorise about their own practice. Experienced teachers can gain access to recent research findings in a way which is relevant to their own concerns and pupils benefit from the fact that the quality of what is being done in schools becomes the focus of attention.

This is not to say that we found the 'right' model for interspersing 'theory' and 'practice'. Indeed, though recent right wing attacks have focused on Initial Teacher Education as failing to get the balance right, our project shows that there are just as many issues to be resolved with experienced teachers. The GAP Group are convinced that an introduction to the project involving 'theory' (a summary of research findings on gender and education, followed by possible explanations) would have turned them off. They wanted to 'do' something and thought they knew 'the theory'. In fact we shared a language but not a common set of understandings about the body of research. As the project progressed, theory was fed in and it seemed to be effective (if somewhat demanding of us, the managers). On the other hand we have subsequently worked on projects which began with 'theory'. In those cases, the responses were positive and teachers claimed that an expectation that they would 'do' something straight away would have turned them off!

More notable perhaps is the empowerment value of teachers learning that *they* are the researchers, that *they* are the experts exploring and managing change, that *their* contribution to making 'theory' is as important as anyone else's and that the theory/practice division especially when used to label people is at least unhelpful and at most, professionally damaging. On this issue we were tough with the group. We did not allow a distinction between the academic and the professional to intrude and where their findings did not match with existing research claims we did not allow them to define themselves as 'wrong' but urged them to ask more questions about why their findings were different. This was a strategy built into the project from the start and it was successful both in terms of building confidence and in maintaining the momentum of work.

The teachers were keen to increase their own professional knowledge and understanding and their interest and confidence grew further as they shared their work with colleagues whom they knew to be interested. The isolation and marginalisation that many teachers experience, when working on equality issues, did not arise. As the project developed, the teachers felt free to comment on their colleagues' work and make suggestions, with the understanding that they were contributing to the overall body of knowledge. As project managers we saw teachers teaching each other, learning from each other and getting really involved with each others' work. In particular, they all began to appreciate the importance of working with a group of teachers from different phases of schooling and the benefits that this could bring. For example, whilst they were able to recognise that the issue of pupil interaction in relation to gender was common to all schools, they were now able to use the expertise and experience of the group members to debate effective and appropriate strategies.

Whilst individual school members were able to meet each other it was an important part of the project that we also met as a whole group. Initially, we believed that this might prove problematic, but decisions were made by the group that the majority of meetings should take place after school in twilight sessions. It was important that all members knew the times and dates of meetings in advance, together with a clear sense of purpose and audience. As project managers we were, on occasions, amazed that after a hard day's teaching the group still had the stamina to engage in such demanding work. It was suggested by the group that it was the existence of firm deadlines together with an awareness of the next stage of the process which moved them forward at such times.

In addition to these meetings, we spent a weekend together (towards the end of the project) when we were able to spend a significant amount of time discussing individual projects and beginning to formally write up the findings. As managers of the project we believe that this time, away from immediate pressures, was essential to teachers being able to clarify their thoughts and was a factor in the project members' decision to try to get their work published. Until this time, we had presumed that our audience would be colleagues in the individual project schools and other interested schools in the Borough, but by the end of the weekend there was a recognition of the need to share their experiences with a wider audience.

The funding for this weekend was allocated from the overall budget allocated to GAP. Additional expenses included consultancy fees for higher education, a limited purchasing of resources such as key texts, photocopying and finance to pay for supply teacher cover. We had initially thought that the provision of finance for the latter would be a significant factor in the success of the project, but this did not turn out to be the case. The teachers were very reluctant to spend much time away from their classes, and in addition there were problems with finding suitable supply cover. What we discovered is that it is not enough just to give money to schools. What is needed is a recognition that time for professional development is properly structured into the school calendar. What is essential is a clear vision on the part of senior management that allocating funds to support individual professional development needs can have a significant impact on the institution.

A model for Professional Development

As managers of the project we believe that as a form of professional development, we found a model which is transferable to most other areas of curriculum development. In the past when teachers have gone out on courses they may or may not have had their needs met. These needs may or may not have been related to the practice in their classrooms and as isolated teachers in individual classrooms, they may have had greater or lesser impact on the overall performance of the school. Furthermore, when they left the school, their expertise often went with them.

In any case, in the light of the dissolution of traditional ways of funding education, the changing role of Local Education Authorities and new procedures for teacher education, a new model will have to be found. Schools will find themselves with increased budgets for staff development and teacher needs identified through the process of appraisal. At the same time many Local Education Authorities, in response to diminishing central budgets, will close central training provision and reduce support staff. In addition, headteachers and governors will need to move their schools forwards as greater demands for improved standards come from central government in the guise of the new inspectorate or the proposed 'hit squads' and as the publication of results begins to take effect. The model of development we have outlined can be undertaken by teachers in clusters of schools linked to 'experts' in the appropriate field, either through institutions of higher education or education consultants. The advantages of this way of working are twofold.

First, the fusion between the theory and the practice is sited in the place where it matters, i.e. with the teachers in their schools. In our experience this creates a momentum and seems to be more successful as a way of changing the culture of the school so that the focus is on learning how to improve and improving how to learn.

Second, in this model none of the 'slippage' described as a feature of past arrangements for INSET can occur since teachers retain control over the content and process of their own professional development needs. It is they who are invited to make suggestions about resolving issues and improving practice in their schools and thus a problem solved for them is a problem solved for the schools.

One unexpected outcome of the project was that over half of those involved have received promotion during the life of the project, either in their own schools or by moving to another institution. We can only assume that this is due to a raising of self awareness on the part of teachers and a recognition of themselves as being professionals in the fullest sense of the term. We believe that involvement on the project gave them the confidence and ability to review their role within education and gain a clearer view of where they wanted to be. What was in fact happening as the teachers asked each other about their work was that they were 'rehearsing their lines' and ensuring a confident response in an interview situation.

Reviewing the project

The authors of each element of the Gender Action Project reached a number of conclusions as outlined in the previous chapters. However, if we make a synthesis of these it would seem that certain patterns emerge. In those schools where all staff were fully aware of the work and where senior management gave support at both a practical and personal level, the projects took root. There was also a greater likelihood that the projects had a deeper, broader and more lasting effect. Ideally the work was part of the overall planning for the school and, as such, was identified in the School's Institutional Development Plan. This was not the case in all of the projects. However, what had been identified in all schools was the need to improve classroom practice and ensure the delivery of a broad, balanced and relevant curriculum for all pupils.

The importance of whole school initiatives in moving practice forward has long been documented, but a consensus about successful strategies to ensure this has not been reached. The need to develop equality policies has been accepted as an important step in changing practice, but following our work we are still faced with the question, 'Which comes first – the policy or the practice?'. Many schools have spent considerable amounts of time consulting with members of the school community and writing policy, but it would seem that only a minority have developed strategies to support policy and undertaken a clear evaluation of the policy's success. In the GAP, schools developed policy and practice at the same time and the policy documents were a result of the work undertaken. In one case the school is yet to complete a written policy but when evaluating its practice it is clear that both staff and pupils are aware of the issues and much progress has been made. In contrast to this the managers of the project are fully aware of many schools with high profile policies but little change in the ethos, curriculum and its delivery.

In the present climate of continual curriculum change, it would seem that many teachers feel unable to develop what they consider to be additional work. Participating in this project has reassured us all that there are many in our schools who do not see equal opportunities as a marginal issue or additional to their everyday practice. They do not see the work to be in conflict with the demands of the National Curriculum but rather, central to its delivery. Issues of curriculum access, delivery and assessment are the topics of conversation in many staffrooms and are the very issues which those working on equality issues have been concerned with for years. Not only can projects be developed and matched on to the National Curriculum, the National Curriculum itself, together with existing legislation can support much of the good work identified by equal opportunities practitioners. The Netley School project, in particular, outlines how a primary school can use its findings to enhance the planning for National Curriculum in subjects such as technology, English and history.

The self selection of the teachers who opted into the GAP suggests, of course, that their enthusiasm and awareness of sex-equality issues was high but even here it is interesting to note the insecurities. Whilst all were experienced and committed, concern and anxiety were expressed about their own competence to deal with equal opportunities issues. Equality practitioners have always acknowledged the need to deploy a variety of strategies when dealing with sensitive issues, ranging from the visionary to the guerrilla. Our experiences support this. Project members found themselves adopting a variety of roles and methodologies. For example, the Reed House project found the use of questionnaires to be less helpful than they had anticipated when trying to establish staff awareness. A more appropriate method turned out to be informal discussion with colleagues. In some cases teachers working on this project identified as a key issue the need to involve a range of staff representing different areas within the school, possessing different roles, experiences and expertise. Teachers who had not worked closely together before found they were able to make a useful contribution to the final outcome. All expressed the importance of a support network both in and outside of their schools. It is interesting to note that in all cases those who had expressed the most commitment to the project were women.

Perhaps the most important finding of the GAP was the confirmation of the need to move beyond having equality issues addressed by teaching staff towards valuing the experiences of children themselves. Whilst this does not seem surprising, it is our belief that many initiatives fail merely because we do not hear what the pupils are telling us. To ignore the pupils' perceptions and experiences of power, sexism and racism is to risk perpetuating inequality and to misunderstand the nature of fundamental changes which must take place in order for equality to be attainable. This project reminds us that the so-called 'bottom up' approach, highlighted by many educators when trying to bring about change, does not start with classroom teachers but with the pupils themselves. We have, for too long, 'done equal opportunities' to the children rather than allowing them to participate in setting the agenda whilst working alongside them. In the light of this it is significant that the most successful projects were those which encouraged children to research the issues for themselves, discover their own strategies and evaluate their findings. This resulted in the children being able to discuss quite sophisticated concepts pertaining to equality and see the relevance of these to their own lives. This must surely be a pointer to more effective means of developing behaviour patterns along non-traditional lines, with children valuing each other as individuals.

The children themselves were able to discuss the issue of single-sex groupings in mixed schools from their own experiences. They examined what they felt and what was happening, not in a theoretical vacuum, but through concrete experiences. Whilst research has indicated positive benefits for girls in single-sex groups, little has been written about similar benefits for boys. However, the Grange Park projects addressed this issue and seem to indicate that further research may well find evidence of advantages for boys too in single-sex groups.

As with other projects, teachers have discovered the need to address a variety of issues not identified initially. In one school, for example, it was discovered that pupil timetabling resulted in exposure to teachers predominantly of one sex. This in itself had not been perceived as particularly relevant until pupils began to talk about their attitudes to teachers, especially with regard to behaviour management. It then became clear that for some pupils the sex of the teacher could be a very significant factor in their day to day experience of teaching and learning.

Whilst the longterm implications of this work are still not clear, the schools acknowledge the importance of the initiative in raising awareness and self-esteem of both staff and pupils and in a number of important ways the work is still continuing. For example, one school subsequently held an open evening to celebrate publicly its commitment to equality of opportunity, its policy and its practice. Another has redesigned its planning processes to ensure equality issues are central to all curriculum developments including content, delivery and assessment. Despite a deluge of demands, schools have indicated both their commitment and ability to move forward on issues of equality of opportunity and the children within these schools can only benefit from this progress.

Introducing the Borough

The Gender Action Project took place in The London Borough of Waltham Forest which is one of the thirty two London Boroughs created in 1965 under the 1963 Local Government Act and is bordered by the London Boroughs of Enfield, Haringey, Hackney, Newham and Redbridge.

The borough is predominantly residential interspersed with areas of industry. The southern part which consists of Walthamstow, Leyton and Leytonstone dates from the nineteenth century and contains two-thirds of the population. It has many of the characteristics of an inner city area, whilst the northern part, containing the inter and post-war properties of Chingford, experiences much less social deprivation.

Waltham Forest is a richly multi-cultural area. In 1991, the census returns indicated that 25.6 per cent of Waltham Forest residents described themselves as black or from an ethnic minority group. The Asian communities are a particular feature of the Borough which contains the largest Pakistani community in London (6.3 per cent with a Bangladeshi community of 0.9 per cent). The largest single group is the Caribbean community (6.8 per cent). Black Africans account for 2.8 per cent with a further 1.75 per cent belonging to Black British or other European groups.

Education

The Council provides four nursery schools, sixty-one primary schools, fourteen secondary schools and six special schools. There are also two sixth form colleges, two grant maintained secondary schools and a College of Further Education in the borough.

The secondary schools are comprehensive schools and teach children up to GCSE level. Of these schools, four are single-sex establishments (two for each sex) and single-sex education for girls is very popular. One of the schools is a Roman Catholic school which is managed by the

Roman Catholic Diocese. This school takes pupils up to the age of eighteen and teaches up to 'A' Level standard.

Equal opportunities

Waltham Forest is a Local Education Authority which has a strong commitment to furthering equality. It is one of the few boroughs to have two education equal opportunities advisers, one with specific responsibility for sex equality the other for race equality. Personnel, both in their roles of employees and 'service deliverers', are informed of the Borough's Equal Opportunities policy on appointment and are encouraged to take personal responsibility for its practical implementation.

The Authority has developed a range of strategies in recent years to highlight race equality and sex equality issues and has supported and encouraged schools and colleges to develop their own policies and practice in order to enhance the educational opportunities of all its learners. A wide range of non-sexist and non-racist materials and resources are available, together with a comprehensive quality programme of professional development training.

In September 1992 the London Borough of Waltham Forest Education Department was presented with a Positive Action Award from the Fawcett Society. This was in recognition of the work undertaken to advance educational opportunities for girls and women. The Fawcett Society believed it to be a well deserved tribute to members of staff ... and to the coherence of the policies and their effective application.

The submission from Waltham Forest included a sample of initiatives undertaken in the Borough's schools and colleges which included a Primary Curriculum Pack - 'When I Grow Up', guidelines for dealing with sexual harassment, a sex equality resource library, a gender equality review and action plan and the Gender Action Project.

APPENDIX B

GENDER ACTION GROUP (notes given to staff in preparation for classroom observation):
Before 'observation' sessions.
1. Read Handout 'What can a classroom do?'
2. Discuss any issues raised from the handout with your partner. e.g.
    (1) Examples of good/bad practice which occur in your classroom/used to occur.
    (2) Any aspects you don't understand or see the relevance of.
    (3) Any strategies you have tried since the Gender Action Group started.

    NB. Think about the classes you will observe. Maybe you will find it easier to observe a class you know/teach.

General Observations

For each section of questions here - read the information in the handout (especially the last 2 paragraphs of 'Talk'.)
    Use the observations you make as starting points for discussion after, and as thoughts for your own teaching.

---

1. LAYOUT
    (a) Where are the boys/girls sitting? Equal spread? Who is in the line of the teacher's vision? (bear in mind teacher movement).
    (b) Have the pupils chosen where to sit, or has the teacher? Does this make a difference?
    (c) Is there equipment in the room? Who is near it?

---

2. TASKS or ACTIVITIES
   (a) What is a typical ratio of boys:girls in a group?
       Have the pupils chosen their group?
   (b) Is there a difference with the way boys and girls use equipment?
   (c) Is there a difference in the 'role' of boys and girls?
       (see pupil: pupil interaction)

---

3. MOVEMENT
   (a) Is there a difference in the way boys and girls move around the room? Does this have an effect on the lesson?

---

4. TALK
   (a) Is the talk 'teacher led'? Is it directive? Short, sharp?
       Is there time for reflection?
   (b) Read the last 2 paragraphs of this section. What can we do?!
       Advice:-

---

5. PUPIL: PUPIL INTERACTION

   (a) How many examples of this stereotyped behaviour do you notice?

Behaviour	No. of Boys	No. of Girls
Competitive		
Co-operating		
'Put down' talk		
Laughing off 'put downs'		
Leaders		
Helpers/carers		
Controlling/directing		
Organising/shaping ideas		
Decision making		
Servicing others		

115

CLASSROOM PRACTICE: GENDER DIFFERENCES

Use this sheet as a tally chart. Try to parallel it with your own experiences.
How long is the observation? _____
Number of girls _____ Number of boys _____
Age of pupils _____

No. of boys featuring frequently		No. of girls featuring frequently	
Teacher asks boy question		Teacher asks girl question	
Boy answers question		Girl answers question	
Boy calls out comment		Girl calls out comment	
Teacher helps boy		Teacher helps girl	
Teacher reprimands boy		Teacher reprimands girl	
Teacher praises boy		Teacher praises girl	

APPENDIX C:

Annual Profile Sheets

CROSS CURRICULAR SKILLS			
NAME:		FORM:	
EXCELLENT	GOOD	ADEQUATE	CAUSING CONCERN
1 SELECTING CONTENT AND STRUCTURING WRITTEN WORK			
Selects what is relevant in given materials and includes original ideas. Always communicates in a range of situations.	Selects relevant content from given materials and sometimes includes original ideas. Can communicate these clearly for most purposes.	Selects relevant content from given materials. Communicates this clearly but simply.	Needs help to select relevant material and/or to organise ideas coherently.
HANDWRITING, SPELLING AND PUNCTUATION			
Sound grasp of spelling and punctuation rules, executed in fluent and legible handwriting.	Is able to communicate accurately and legibly.	Has mastered handwriting techniques, spelling of key words and basic sentence construction.	Has difficulties in one or more of (a) letter formation; (b) spelling basic words; (c) constructing simple sentences.
3 CONTRIBUTING TO AND FOLLOWING DISCUSSION			
Articulate and confident. Can inform and persuade. Shows listening skills through comments and questions on child and teacher statements and through body language.	Tries to contribute even when unsure. Generally communicates clearly. Appropriacy of information and opinions offered indicates good listening skills. Understands 'turn taking'.	Listens quietly. Contributes to class when confident, has something to offer. Full participant in group work.	(1) Does not listen to others: chats or tries to dominate discussion or (2) Reluctant to participate. Contributes only when asked directly to do so or (3) Responses indicate difficulty in following main points in discussions.

CROSS CURRICULAR SKILLS			
NAME:		FORM:	
EXCELLENT	GOOD	ADEQUATE	CAUSING CONCERN
4 LISTENING TO AND FOLLOWING INFORMATION			
Can carry out tasks from complex instructions. Can concentrate for a considerable length of time on teacher and pupils, follow main points and detail in information and stories and use these in discussion or writing without additional help.	Can carry out tasks from complex instructions. Can usually concentrate as long as is required, follow main points in information and stories and rarely needs repetition in order to use these in discussion or writing.	Can carry out tasks from simple, clear instructions. Can concentrate for a reasonable length of time and follow main points in information given or in a story, though may sometimes need to check items or require clarification.	(1) Poor concentration, fidgets, chats or daydreams. (2) Needs individual help and frequent repetition in order to understand instructions and information given orally.
5 MEMORY RECALL			
Recalls easily and clearly both in short and long term. Can learn by heart or recall gist as appropriate.	Good short term memory and, with revision, recalls a considerable amount in tests.	Within a carefully structured learning programme can recall main points.	Poor recall even when making an effort.
6 OBSERVATION			
Sees relevance of observations to the problem at hand. Notices the unusual/intangible. Sees the whole as well as parts.	Notices detail. Is highly accurate.	Can make obvious observations.	Needs guidance to make even obvious observations.
7 READING			
Can read fluently and for gist with total understanding from a variety of sources.	Can read with understanding from a variety of texts.	Can read and understand an appropriate text and instructions.	Needs teacher guidance to recognise words and/or understand meaning of simple text.
8 RESEARCH SKILLS			
Can investigate problems using a wide range of materials from outside school as well as in.	Can locate and use information from several different school sources to solve a given problem.	Can locate a relevant book independently using library system and find information using index to solve a given problem.	Can select appropriate information only with careful guidance.

CROSS CURRICULAR SKILLS			
NAME:		FORM:	
EXCELLENT	GOOD	ADEQUATE	CAUSING CONCERN
9 WORKING IN A GROUP			
Can organise tasks and initiate ideas, listen to others, help develop Ideas and hold group together.	Works cooperatively and can contribute and develop ideas.	Cooperates with others. Carries out given tasks reliably. Tries to contributes ideas.	(1) Unwilling to negotiate - wants own way; or (2) little contribution made; or (3) behaviour undermines group.
10 WORKING INDEPENDENTLY			
Shows initiative, motivation and interest. Has enough mastery of learning skills and confidence to work alone.	Capable of solid work with little additional help. Usually produces what is required with some style.	With clear guidance can fulfil a set task.	(1) Needs/demands constant guidance and help; (2) Applies self only under supervision.
11 PROBLEM SOLVING			
Can construct original solutions, devise tests and/or experiments to check hypotheses, apply relevant knowledge to any problems.	Can interpret and understand problem, follow steps in an argument or method in a problem.	Can employ a learned method to solve similar problems.	(1) Needs help to under-stand/interpret problem. Finds it difficult to use given method to solve problems. (2) Gives up easily.
12 PHYSICAL CO-ORDINATION			
Fine and gross motor skills well-developed. Can perform varied practical tasks accurately and with ease.	Can co-ordinate physical movements to carry out practical activities for given tasks.	Can co-ordinate physical movements to carry out practical activities for given tasks.	(1) Needs help to perform practical tasks. (2) Needs to exercise more control. Sometimes unsafe.
13 COMPUTING SKILLS			
Can use Load, Save & Print independently and at appropriate times. Quickly grasps use of new software. Understands potential of computers and can suggest applications across the curriculum.	Understands how and when to use Load, Save & Print and can use these to carry out given tasks. Confident in use of familiar software and needs little explanation to use new items.	Can Load, Save & Print work when told to do so. Can use familiar software, but needs full explanation to use new items.	Needs help to make computer perform any of its functions. Does not carry what has been learned into new situations, carries out tasks by rote rather than understanding.

CROSS CURRICULAR SKILLS			
NAME:	FORM:		
EXCELLENT	GOOD	ADEQUATE	CAUSING CONCERN
14 NUMERACY			
Draws from a wide range of numerical tools to recognise and apply appropriate solutions.	Can apply a range of mathematical activities with some guidance.	Can apply the rules of computation in various circumstances.	Has trouble using rules of computation.

APPENDIX D

SELECTION OF QUESTIONS AND ANSWERS FROM THE VIDEO
EVENING QUESTIONNAIRE

What do you think you learned from the Gender Action Project?

How to work in groups (several children wrote this)
What goes on in different classes
How to cooperate
How people are treated and how they respond
Differences in girls' and boys' behaviour 'Not to be sexist + girls and boys are the same' (a boy)
How boys and girls react to each other
'I built up my confidence' (a boy)

Do you notice things about gender more than you did before the project?

'Boys tend to be louder and use more violence than girls do' (a girl)
'Yes' (several children simply wrote 'yes'!)
'Yes, I have noted that girls and boys still don't mix that much'
'Yes, I noticed that girls and boys play together. More than I thought.'
'Yes, we didn't know anything about gender before the project' (one of the most disruptive boys)
'Yes, I did. I didn't really know that boys did less tidying up than girls' (a boy)

Do you notice anything about gender in your new school or class? Give details

'As I am in a girls' school, I find that I have more opportunities than boys. There are lots of issues about famous women I did not know about'.

'I think if we did it again our results would be the same'.

'Some children still haven't changed and they treat their opposite sex abusively'.

'People are mature. Boys and girls do talk with each other'.

Do you think you ever behave differently because of what you learned from GAP? If so, how and when?

'Yes. In PE when you are put to work with a girl I am not sexist because I learnt that girls can do things better than boys and boys can do things better than girls'.

'Yes, but only a little bit. Maybe I've said some things I shouldn't have, but I realise now' (a boy) 'I think I've changed because I think I can work in mixed groups.'

'A little bit' (Many children wrote this).

'I learned that it is better to mix and cooperate so now I do more than before'

'I hang around with girls more because I learnt from the GAP' (one of more disruptive boys).

Bibliography

Anti-Sexist Working Party (1985) '"Look Jane, Look": Anti-Sexist initiatives in Primary Schools' in (ed) Weiner, G. *Just a Bunch of Girls*, London, OU Press, pps. 134–145.

Askew and Ross (undated) *Anti-sexist materials for boys*. ILEA.

Askew, S. and Ross, C. (1988) *Boys Don't Cry: Boys and sexism in education* London: Open University Press; Gender in Education Series.

Brah, A. and Minhas, R. (1985) 'Structural Racism or Cultural Difference: Schooling for Asian Girls' in (ed) Weiner, G. *Just a Bunch of Girls*. London: OU Press, pps. 14–25.

Bryan, B., Dadzie, S. and Scafe, S. (1987) 'Learning to Resist: black women in education' in (eds) Weiner, G. and Arnot, M. *Gender Under Scrutiny*. London: Hutchinson: pps. 90–100.

Cant, A. (1985) 'Development of LEA Policy: Manchester' in (eds) Whyte, J., Dean, R. and Cruickshanks, M. *Girl Friendly Schooling*. London: Methuen, p.149.

Clarricoates, K. (1987) 'Dinosaurs in the Classroom - the "hidden" curriculum in primary schools' in (eds) Arnot, M. and Weiner, G. *Gender and the Politics of Schooling*. London: Hutchinson, pps. 155–165.

Freeman, K. (1992) *Journey to West Africa*, video, Waltham Forest Local Education Authority.

Kelly, A. (1987) 'The Construction of Masculine Science' in (eds) Arnot, M. and Weiner, G. *Gender and the Politics of Schooling*. London: Hutchinson, pps. 127–138.

Kruse, A.M. (1992) '"We have learnt not to just sit back, twiddle our thumbs and let *them* take over." Single-sex settings and the development of a pedagogy for girls and a pedagogy for boys in Danish schools' in (eds) *Gender and Education: Women's Education in Europe*. Vol. 4 Nos. 1&2 pps. 81–103

Lees, S. (1987) 'The Structure of Sexual Relations in School' in (eds) Arnot, M. and Weiner, G. *Gender and the Politics of Schooling*. London: Hutchinson, pps. 183–185.

Mahony, P. (1989) 'Sexual Violence in Mixed Schools' in (eds) Jones, C. and Mahony, P. *Learning our Lines*. London: The Women's Press, p.174.

Mahony, P. (1985) *Schools for the Boys: Co-education reassessed*. London: Hutchinson.

Meighan, R. (1987) *A Sociology of Educating*. London: Holt, pps. 66–67 and 302–312.

Millman, V. (1987) 'Teacher as Researcher: A new tradition for research on gender' in (eds) Weiner, G. and Arnot, M. *Gender Under Scrutiny*. London: Hutchinson, p. 258.

Myers, K. (1987) *Genderwatch*. London: SCDC Publishers.

Spender, D. and Sarah, E. (eds) (1980) *Learning to Lose*. London: The Women's Press.

Spender, D. (1982) *Invisible Women: The Schooling Scandal*. London: Writers' and Readers' Co-operative.

Stanworth, M. (1987) 'Girls on the Margins: a study of gender divisions in the classroom' in (eds) Weiner, G. and Arnot, M. *Gender under Scrutiny*. London: Hutchinson, pps. 198–212.

Taylor, H. (1985) 'Inset for Equal Opportunities in the London Borough of Brent' in (eds) Whyte, J., Dean, R., & Cruickshanks, M. *Girl Friendly Schooling*, Methuen, p.105.

Walden, J. (1990) *Gender Issues in Classroom Organisation and Management*, London Borough of Waltham Forest.

Weiner, G. (1990) 'Developing Educational Policy on Gender in the Primary School: The Contributions of Teachers in the United Kingdom' in (ed) Weiner, G. *The Primary School and Equal Opportunities*. London: Cassell, pps. 35–51.

Index